Status! Status! Status!

Exhibition & Workshop for International Artists

12/16/2011 – 12/18/2011

Artists Included

Sarah Butler
Noa Charuvi
Yunwoo Choi
Tamar Ettun
Allison Freeman w/ Tara Kelton
Elisa Garcia de la Huerta
Wieteke Heldens
Zeynab Izadyar
Hwan Jahng
Gelare Khoshgozaran
Jung ah Kim
Eun Jin Kim
Grace Kim
Julie Lænkholm
Catherine Chiao Ju Lan
Adehla Lee
Shiyuan Liu
Sanaz Mazinani
Uno Nam
Astrid Nobel
Jong Oh
Iliana Ortega
Hayal Pozanti
Nooshin Rostami
Naomi Safran-Hon
Alexandra Wolkowicz

For more Information visit:
ag-wf.com/status/

Hosted at: Interstate Projects

Exhibition

The exhibition champions the accomplishments and impending struggles of international artist currently residing in New York. The gloom of administrative and quotidian preoccupations can make the life of artists brash and tiresome. Depending on the circumstances of each artist, achieving status and recognition in the U.S. can injure the development of creativity. Status! Status! Status! signals a superficial difference between friends, which can be overcome.

It is then the goal of this exhibition to present friends with cordiality. A respect for amity results in a tolerance of stylistic dis-ambiguities. Therefore, we present work from individuals sharing in a common contingency. The works exhibited will radiate not only with the poetics of their appearance, but with commonalities that perforate the daily life of their authors.

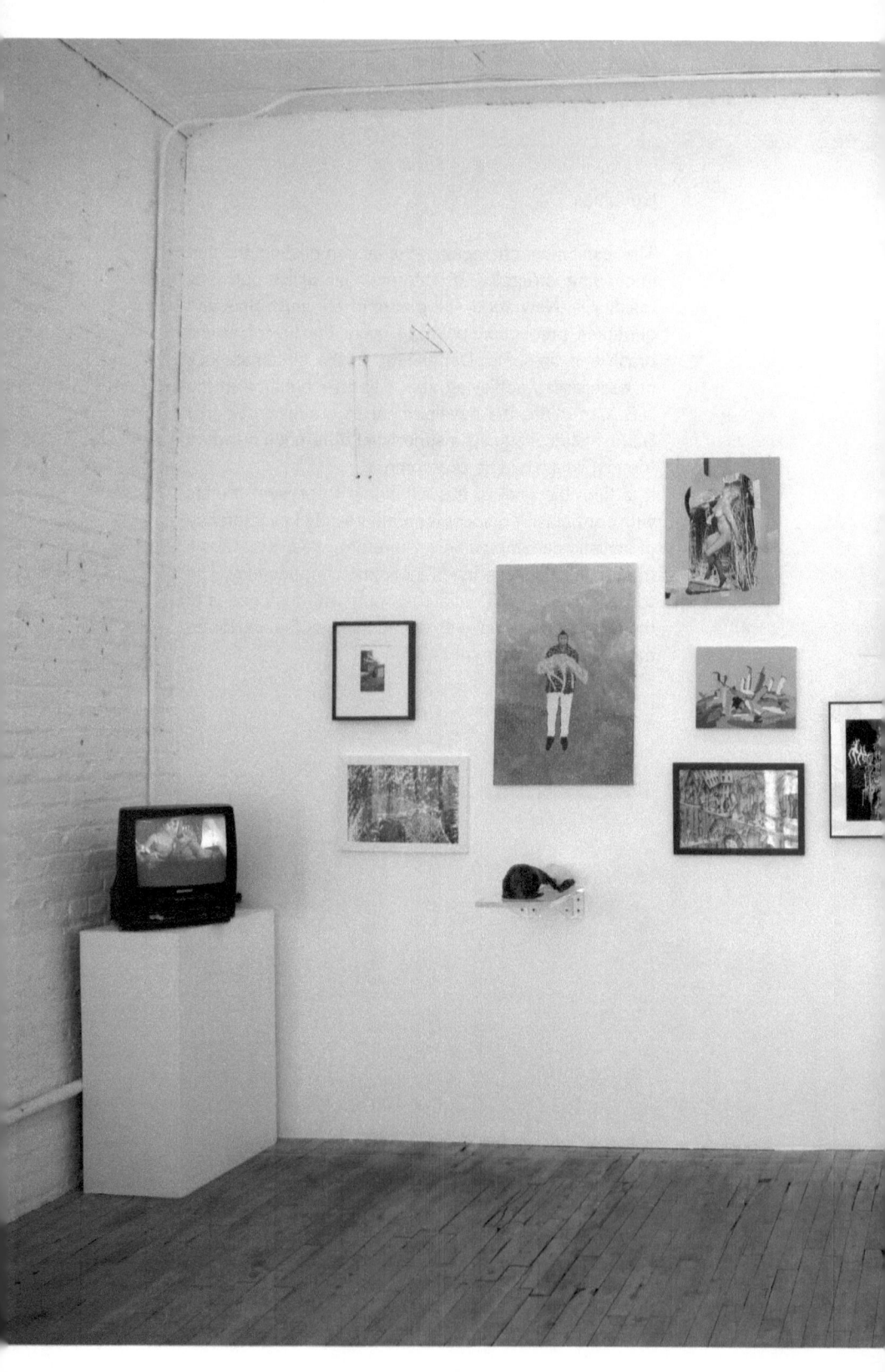

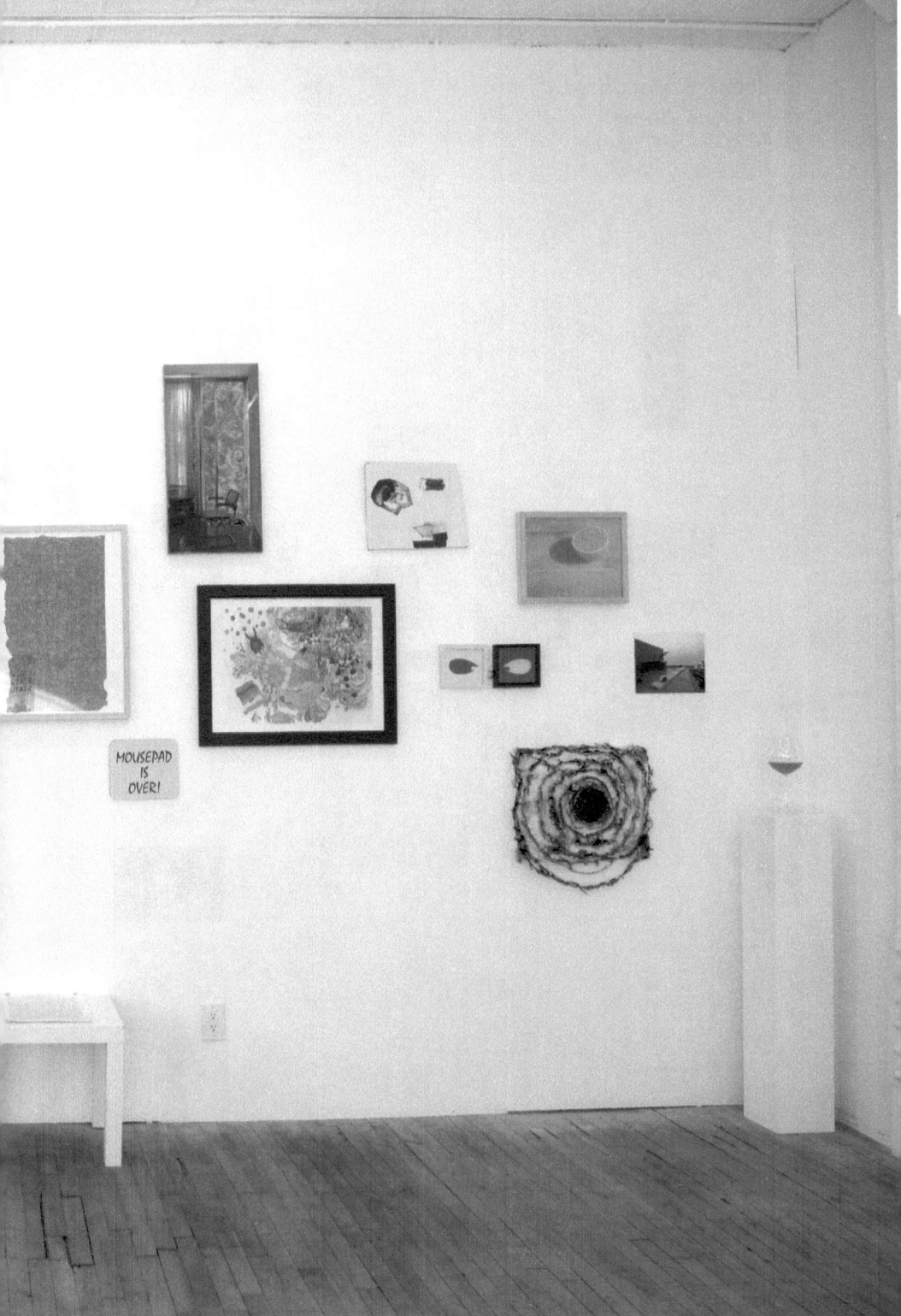

<u>Status! Status! Status!</u>

Exhibition & Workshop for
International Artists
December 16–18, 2011

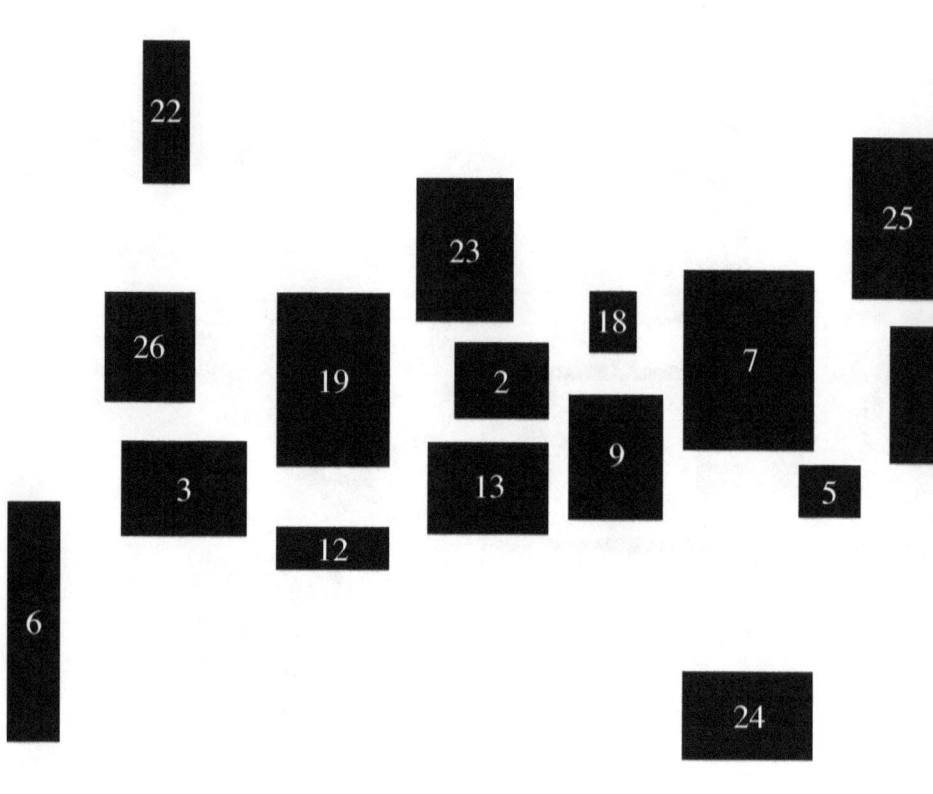

1. Sarah Butler
2. Noa Charuvi
3. Yunwoo Choi
4. Tamar Ettun
5. Allison Freeman
   with Tara Kelton

6. Elisa Garcia de la Huerta
7. Wieteke Heldens
8. Zeynab Izadyar
9. Hwan Jahng
10. Gelare Khoshgozaran
11. Jungah Kim

12. Eun Jin Kim
13. Grace Kim
14. Catherine Chiao-Ju Lan
15. Julie Laenkholm
16. Adehla Lee
17. Shiyuan Liu

Interstate Projects Presents
Curated and Organized by AGWF

56 Bogart Street
Brooklyn, NY 11206

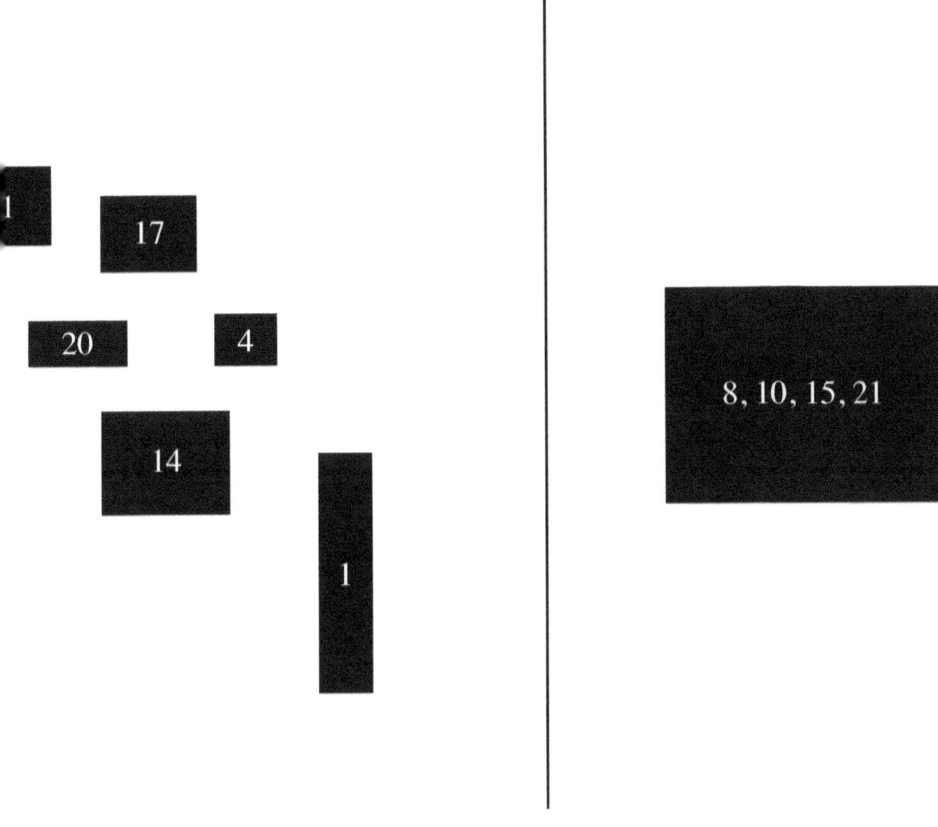

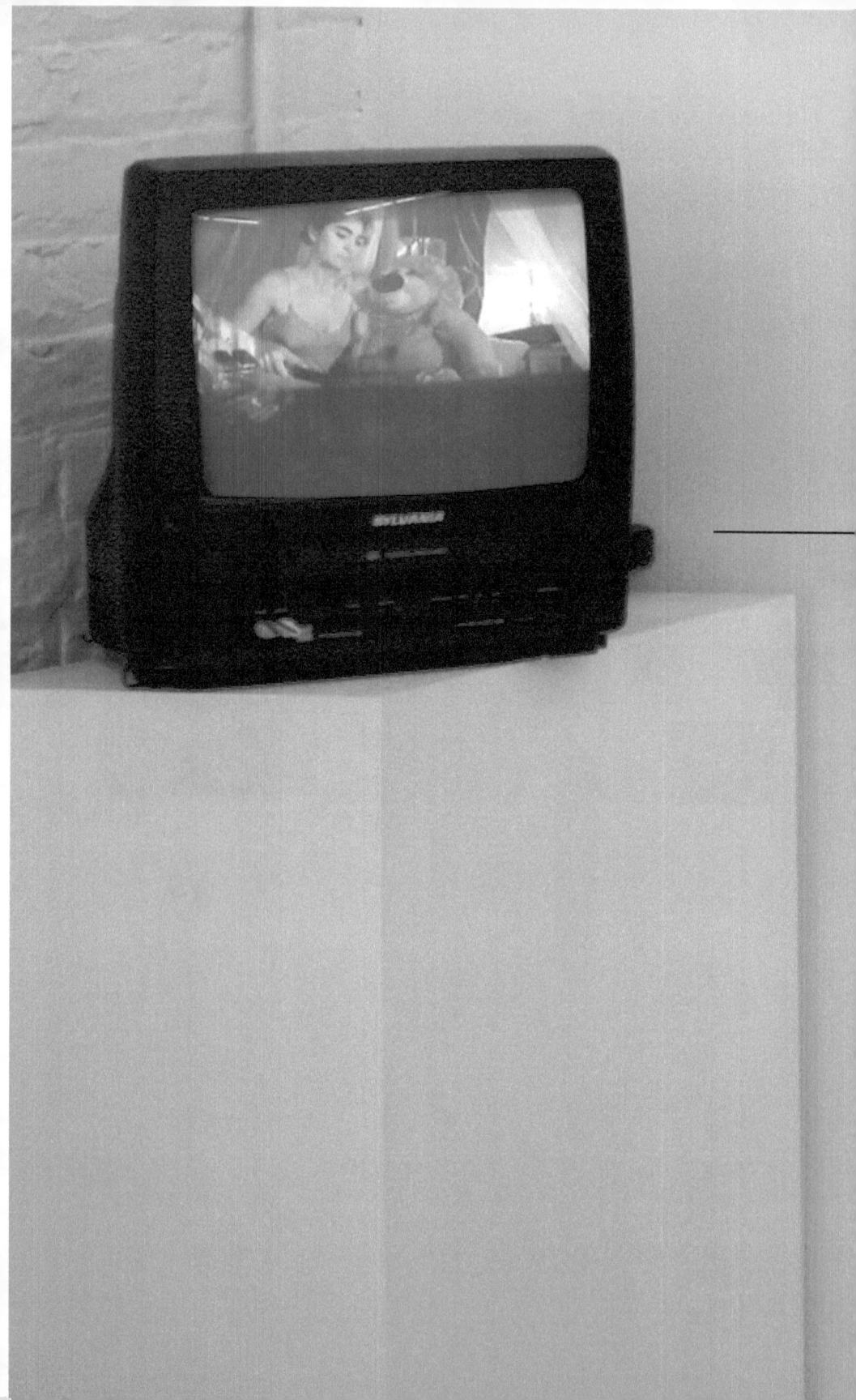

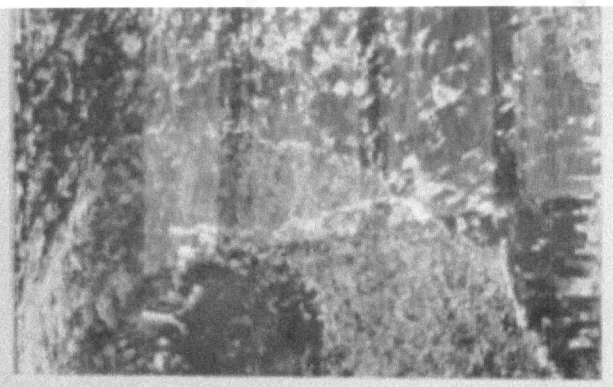

Elisa Garcia de la Huerta
The honeymoon
video
25*25

Creating a set of rules where in One Week I will
perform a series of stereotypical episodes of my
childish quintessential ideal fairytale of a honeymoon,
in The Honeymoon I will expose myself, being open
to circumstances of contradictions and a encumbered
assortment of emotions in a "relationship": between
my "grown up Teddy Bear" (big stuffed animal)
and the self. The 15 min video presents, in it's own
process: simplicity, capricious feelings, maternity, care,
frustration, attraction, desire, objectivity and an under
layer of loneliness and subjectivity. I use video and
photography to document the performance of personal
experiences in secret spaces, uncovering profound
struggle, fear, anger, anxiety, sadness and pain. The
emotional gaps of loss, instability and balance exist
within vulnerability. Through an intuitive process of
poised intensity, I discover and repair these lapses in
spaces of concealment and juxtaposition.

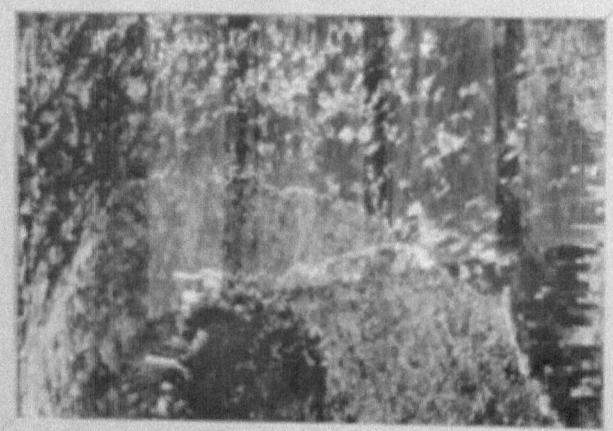

Yun-Woo Choi
Just Another Day
Photo
17*13

What is real? Am I living in the plane or
dimension that I thought what it is? In my
life, some of my feelings seem to have no
reasonable cause, and there are no divisions
between spiritual and secular ideas, slight
and deep feelings. Because of my endless
dualistic conceptualizing, my mind which
is originally seamless oneness is divided
into numerous fragments. I want to reveal
the spaces hidden beyond the dualistic
conception which always accompanies
symbolic language through my work.

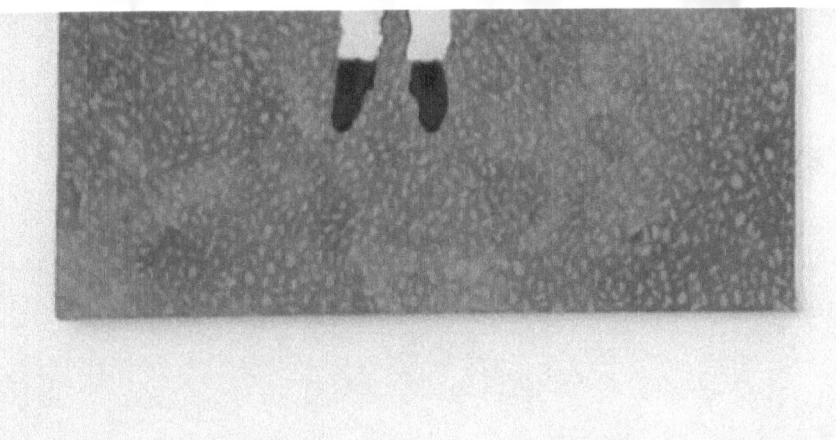

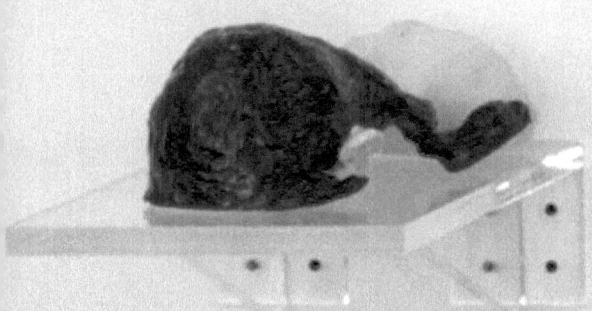

Eun Jin Kim
Qual-la
Glazed Stoneware
12*5

It is about a drunken
girl in the process of
black out.

Alexandra Wolkowicz
Outside with Mama
Digital c-type print
12*14
(This print is 1 of 15 photos from the series 'Time Windows')

TIME WINDOWS
Squaring up to the past
This series of photographs was taken in November 2009 while
my father was moving out of his flat in Weilbergstr. 1 where I
grew up. Whilst helping to pack I looked again at old photographs
and began to map the past with the present. I became the viewer
and the viewed. 'Time Windows' has been exhibited as part of a
touring show, 'Home and Away', at Fringe Arts in Bath (UK) and
Castlefield gallery, Manchester in 2010. The group show is
currently exhibited at ISE Cultural Foundation in NYC.

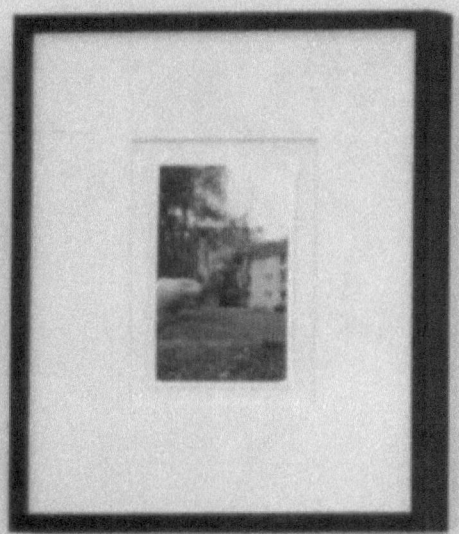

Uno Nam
The Death of Golden Calf
Acrylic Paints
20*30

The golden calf never dies. ⌐

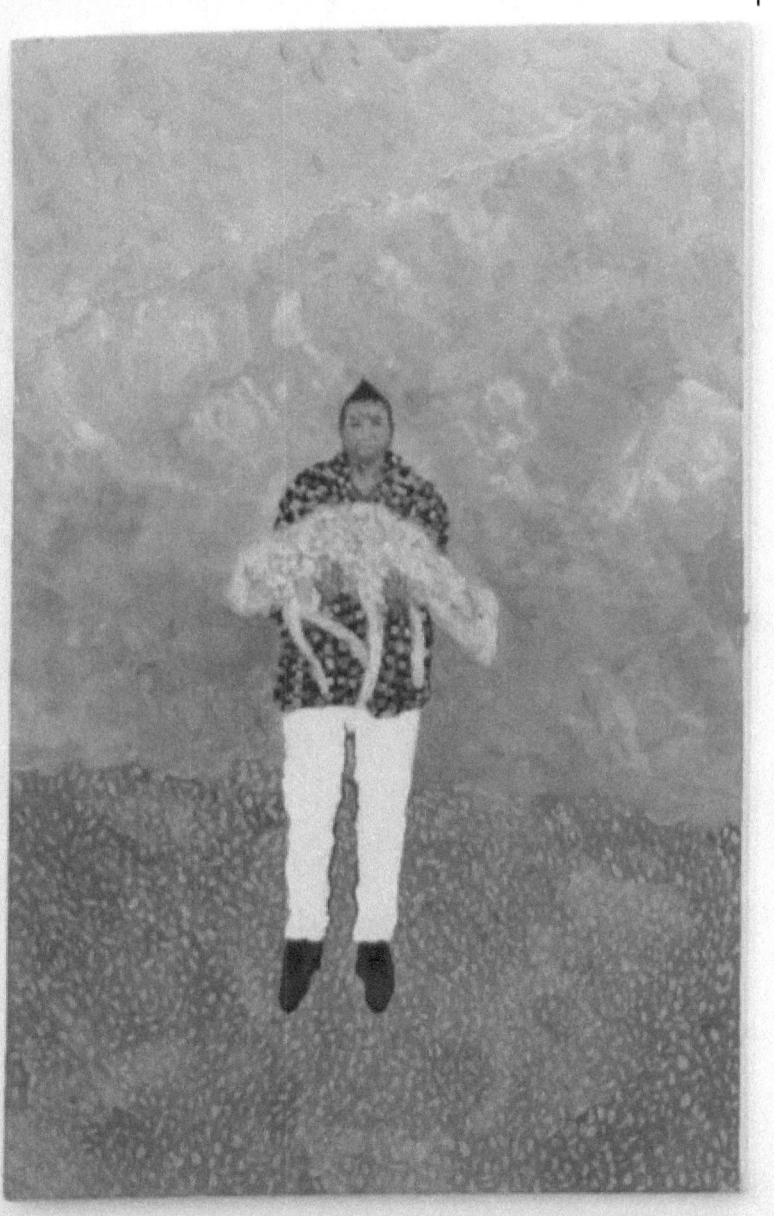

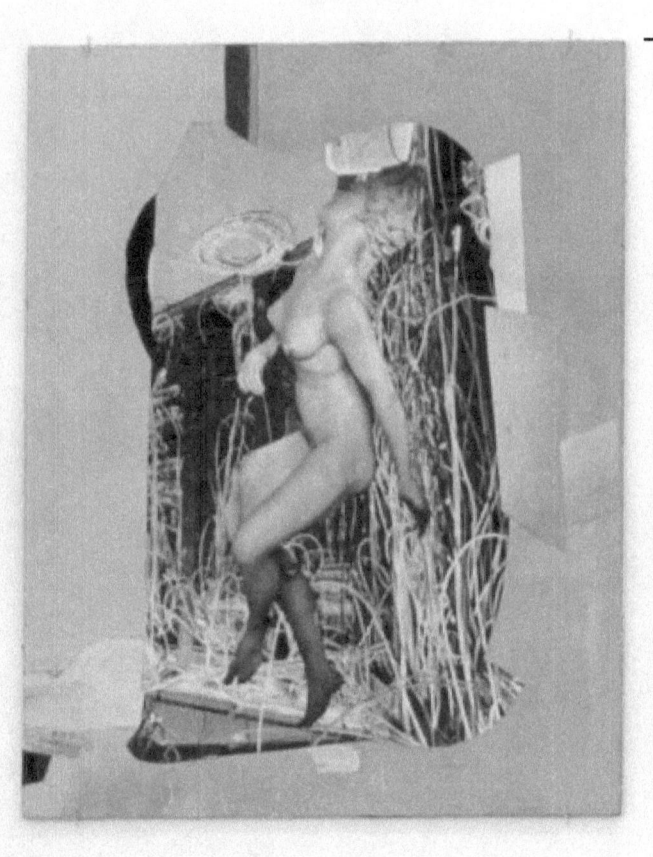
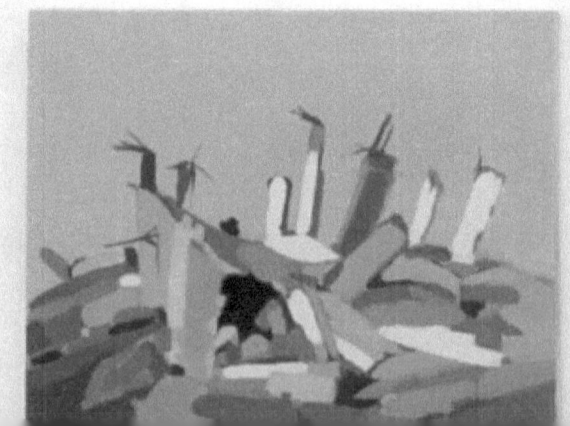

Hayal Pozanti
Merging
Collage
12.75*16.5

The Singularity is close - we
become the cloud and the cloud
becomes us. Soon, the earth will
be a landscape of server rooms.

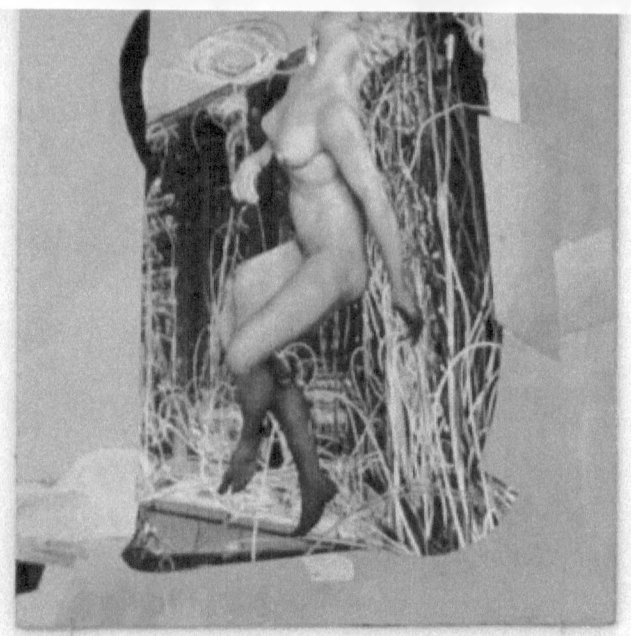

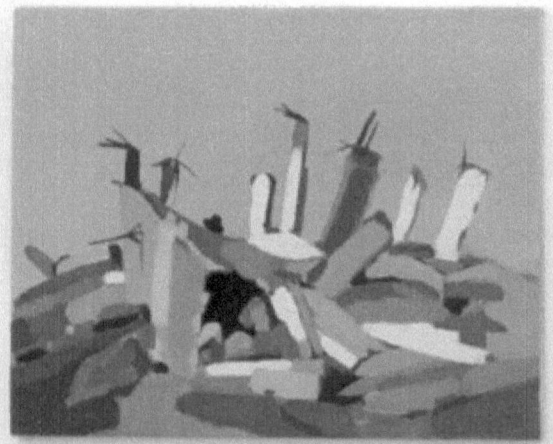

Noa Charuvi
Pink Path
Oil on canvas
mounted on panel
14*11

based on a photograph
of a bombed building
in Gaza.

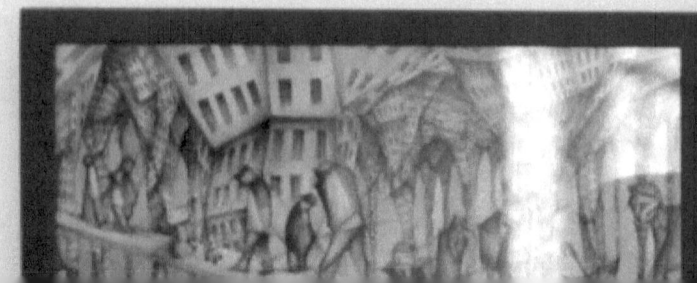

Sanaz Mazinani
RQ-170 Sentinel drone
Embossment on paper
5.5*7.5

I made this work as a direct response to the United States' secret
surveillance effort of Iran that was revealed by the crash of a drone
on Dec 4th, 2011. The stealth C.I.A. drone, was a bat winged
RQ-170 Sentinel that was reportedly spotted over northern Iran
and was brought down via cyber attack to a safe landing 155
miles from the Afghanistan border. "RQ-170 Sentinel" is an
embossment made on paper. A form of etching without ink, the
technique produces raised portions on the surface of paper. I
chose this technique for its presence. For me, the relief, white-on-
white image, alludes to the undercover aspects of a spy operation
and U.S. military tactics. I am always thinking about U.S. foreign
policy and how the standards its sets effect the lives of individual
citizens. This work is a quiet nod to my acknowledgement of the
U.S. espionage hostilities against Iran.

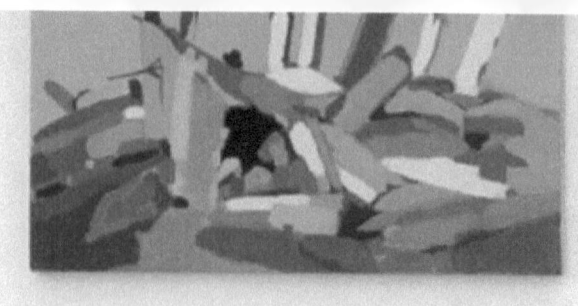

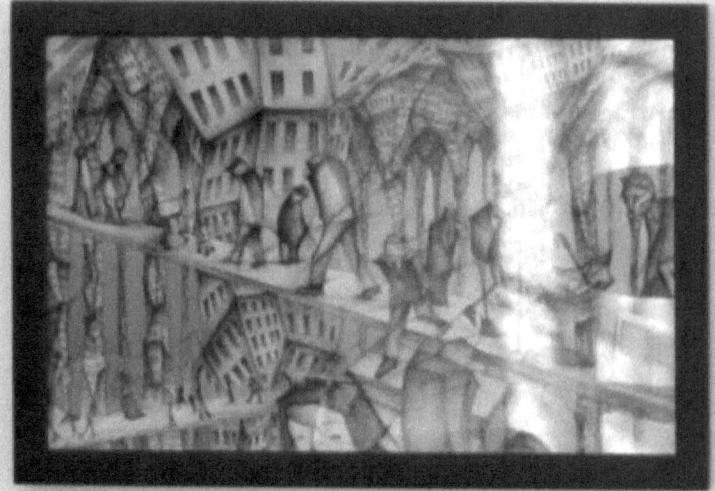

Grace Kim
The City
Pencil
19*13

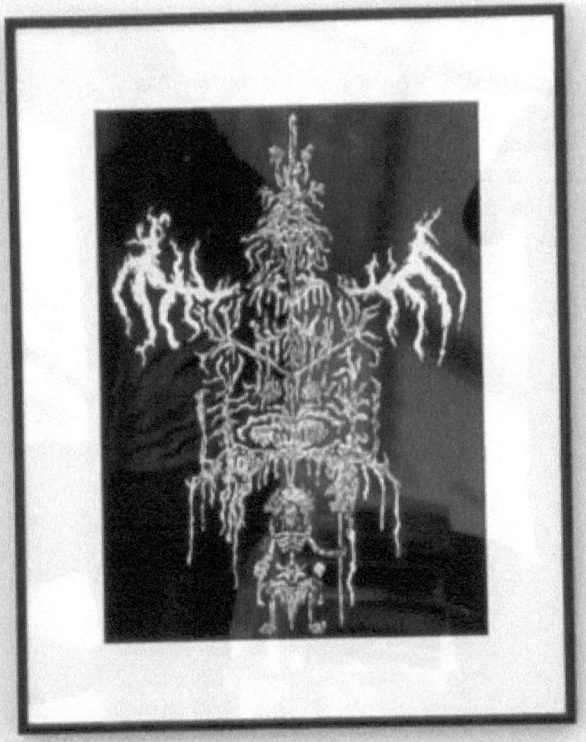

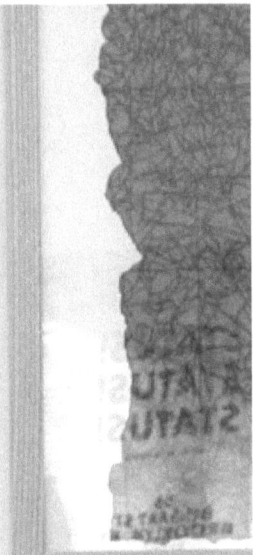

Hwan Jahng
Summoning No.1
Gouache on Paper
15*19

The very first piece of the series of Metal-
inspired works. Though listening to it for
more than ten years, I had never made any
pieces before, infused with my passion as a
fan of this music and its culture. It is also
noteworthy that it marked a departure from
using photograph as a source material. I
have started to directly access my mind and
vision and visualize it after making this piece.

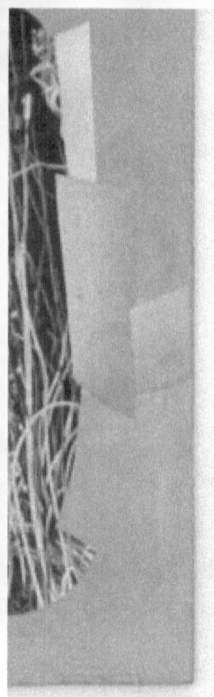

Wieteke Heldens
I am sorry, No content
Marker on brown bag
18*24

What you see are the wrinkles of the brown bag.
Heldens' took the content out. The lines tell you the
future like reading the palm of your hand, but at the
same time they show you the scars of the past. These
works hint at the conflicting desires to both suppress
and emote raw desires and irrational needs.

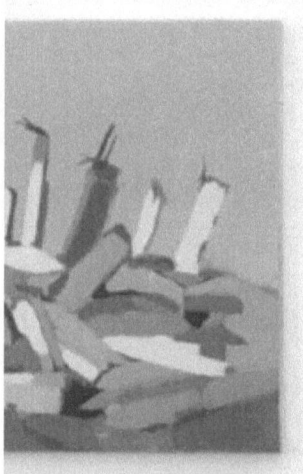

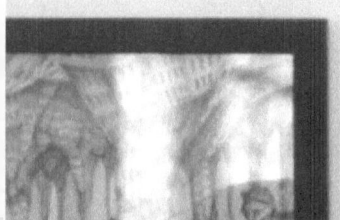

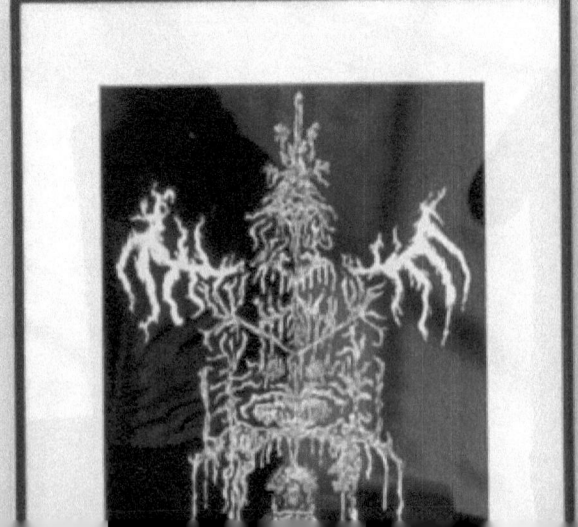

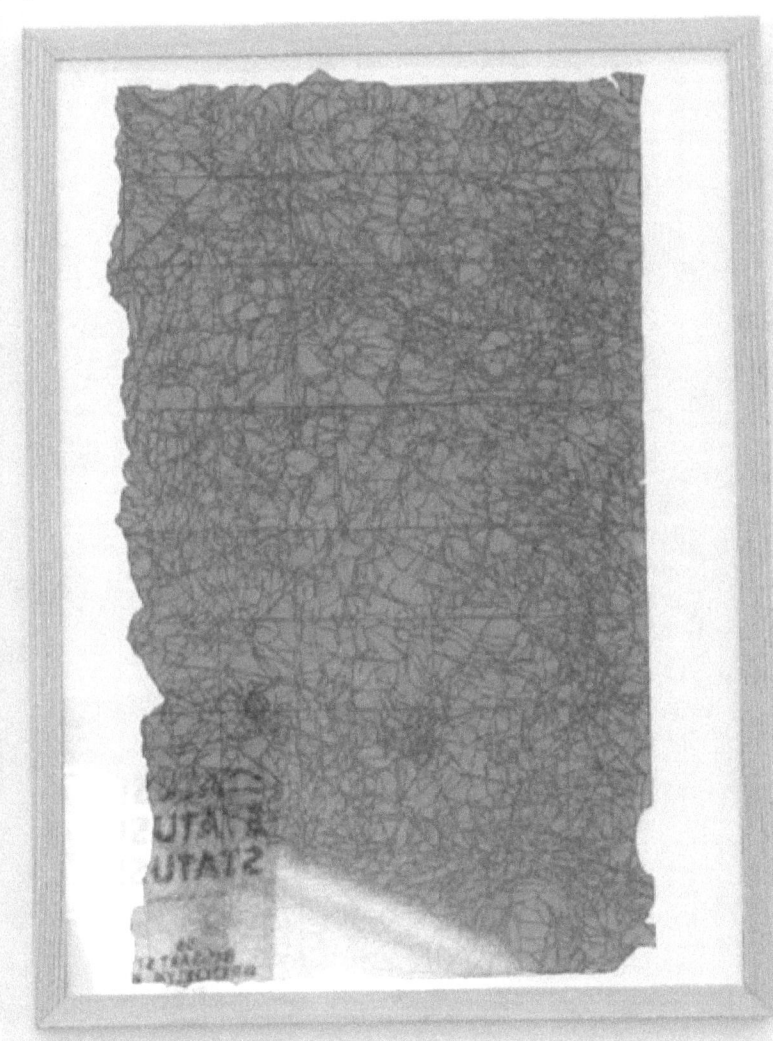

MOUSEPAD

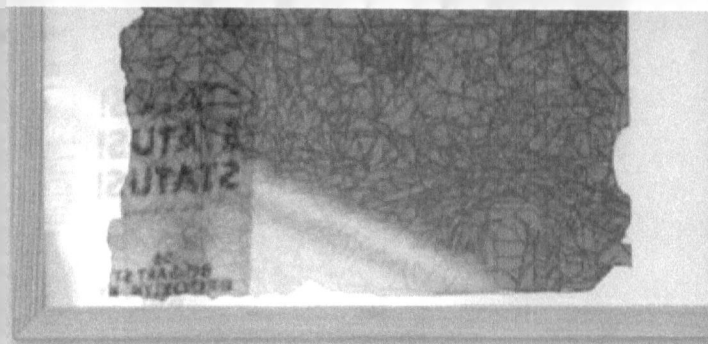

MOUSEPAD
IS
OVER!

Allison Freeman / Tara Kelton
Mousepad is Over!
Mousepad
9.25*7.75

Announcing the death of this mousepad.

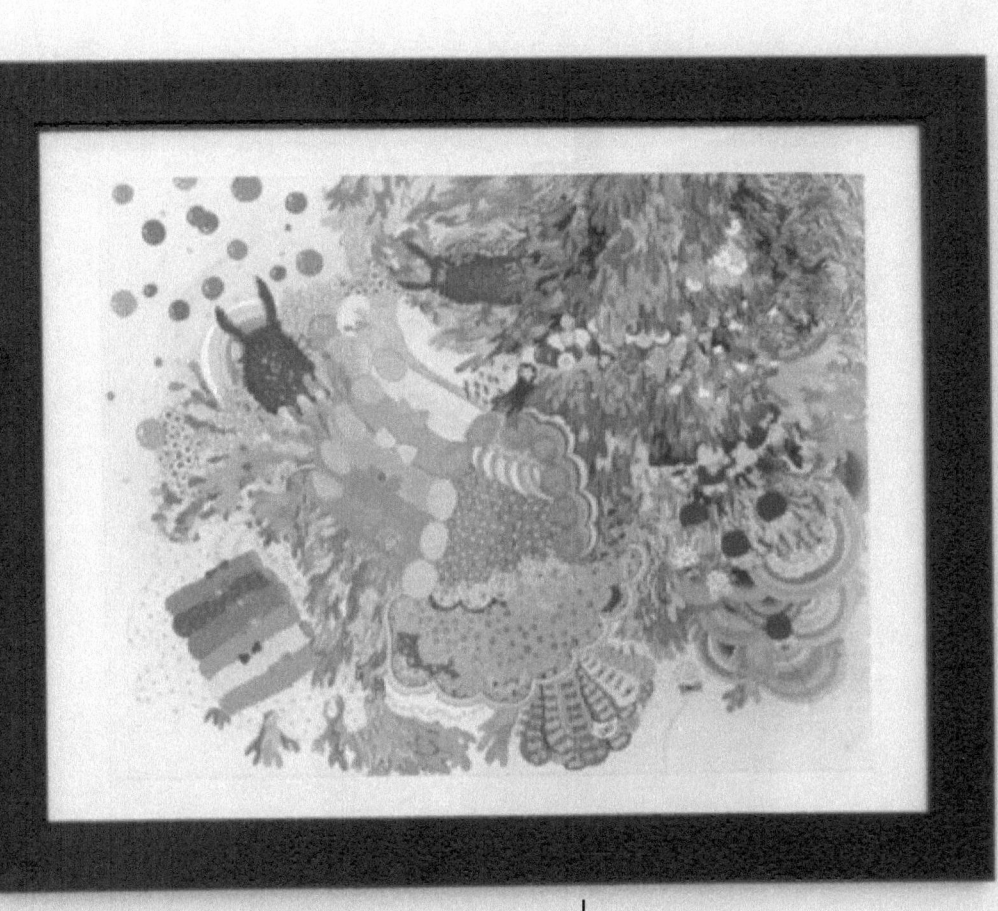

Adehla Lee
31577-10024
Acrylic on Paper
20*15

This is drawing illustrates the
visual experience of something
that is festive and serious at the
same time.

Naomi Safran-Hon
Home Invasion X
Archival ink jet print, lace and cement on canvas
13*25

An image of a home is destroyed and rebuild through the creative
process. The photographic image is interrupted with the use of
cement and lace thus creating a new reality.

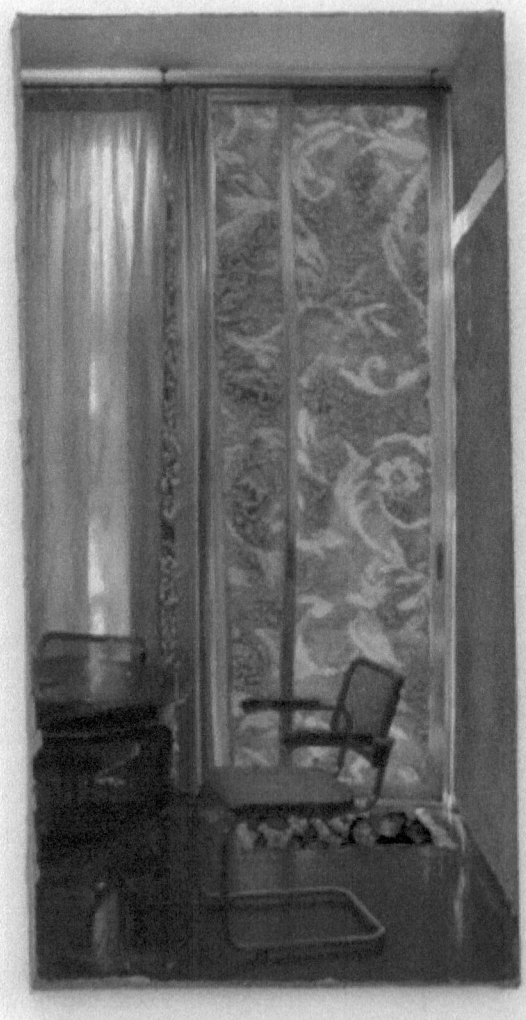

Name Jung ah Kim
EIGHT
Acrylic on wood
12*14
EIGHT is 8TH piece of a 12 panel set. This series is basically consisted of 2 parts; carving which includes cutting the wood board and painting. First, I cut and carved wood panels following certain rules about shapes and numbers that I set somewhat mathematically. For the painting part, I worked on each panel for short amount of time (5 minute to less than 1 hour max) to study effectively subtle change of my reaction to the elements of the base panel as I move on to one after another. It's like a document of building relationship among works, artist, and given circumstance.

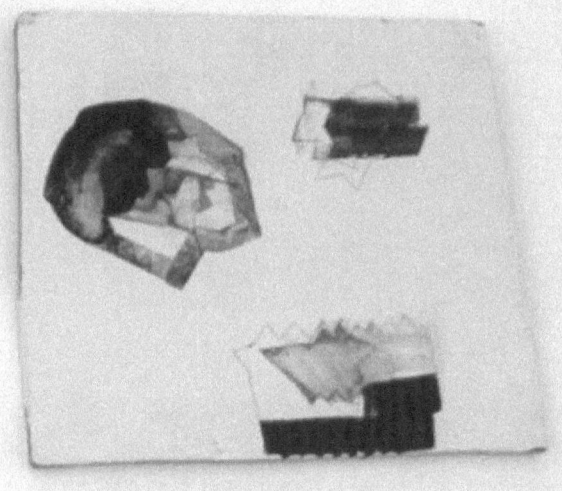

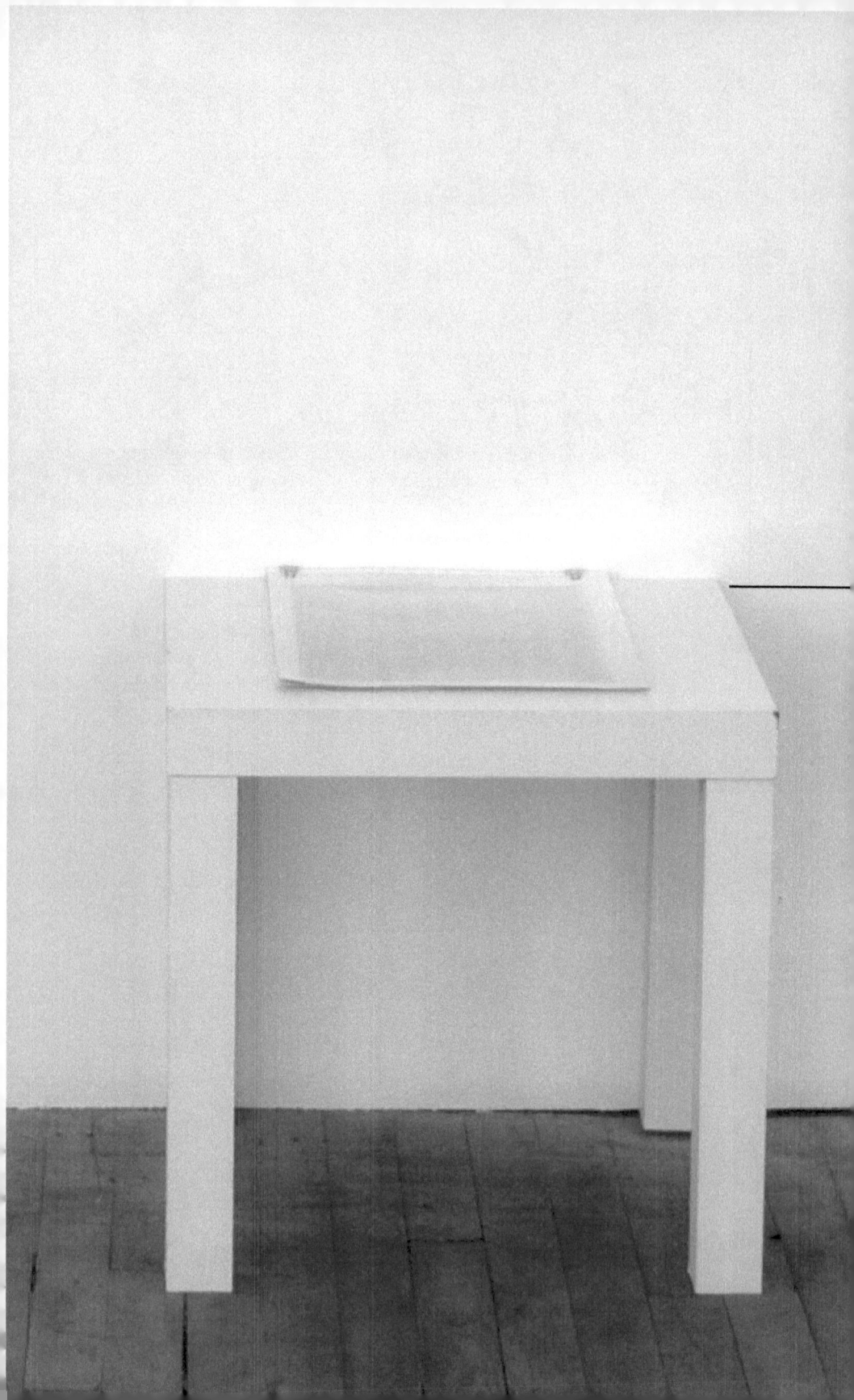

Nooshin Rostami
Distitled
Mixed media
11*17
This artwork is not
well presented for a
show in a gallery.

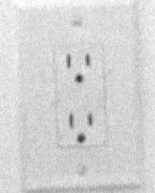

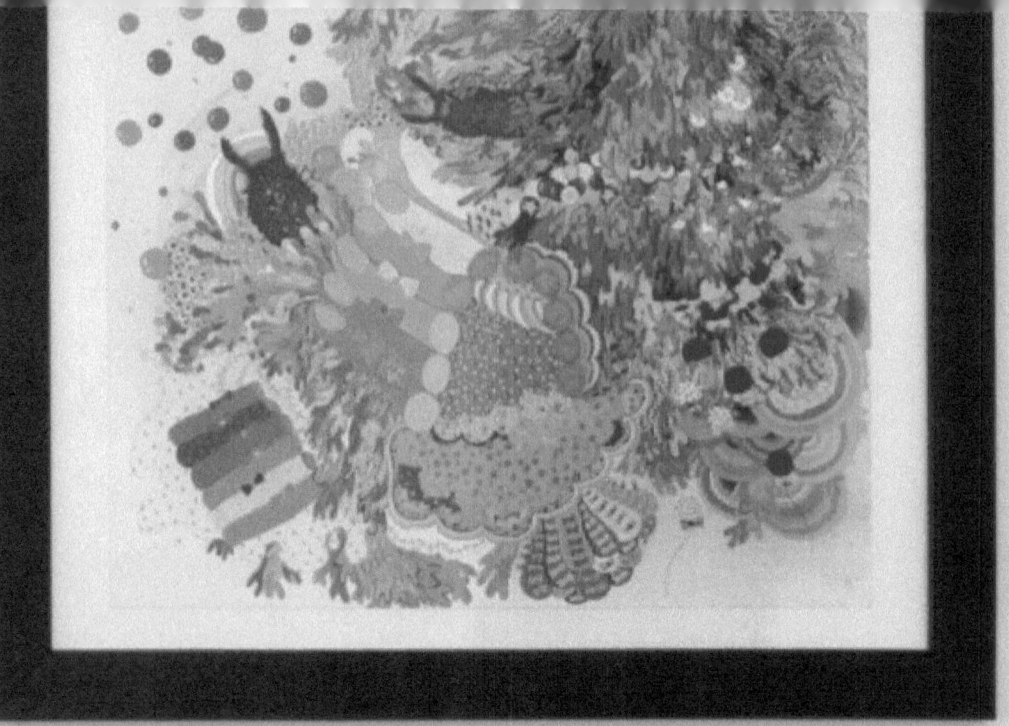

Astrid Nobel
Inter et Inter: an Interlude
Medium cartonboard cutouts, framed and connected
14*5.7

The work is a work between works; sketching a period of being in between decisions while facing contradictory possibilities. Inter et Inter (between and between) was used by Kierkegaard in Either/Or to illustrate the aesthetic individual making a distinction between what accidentally and essentially belongs to him.

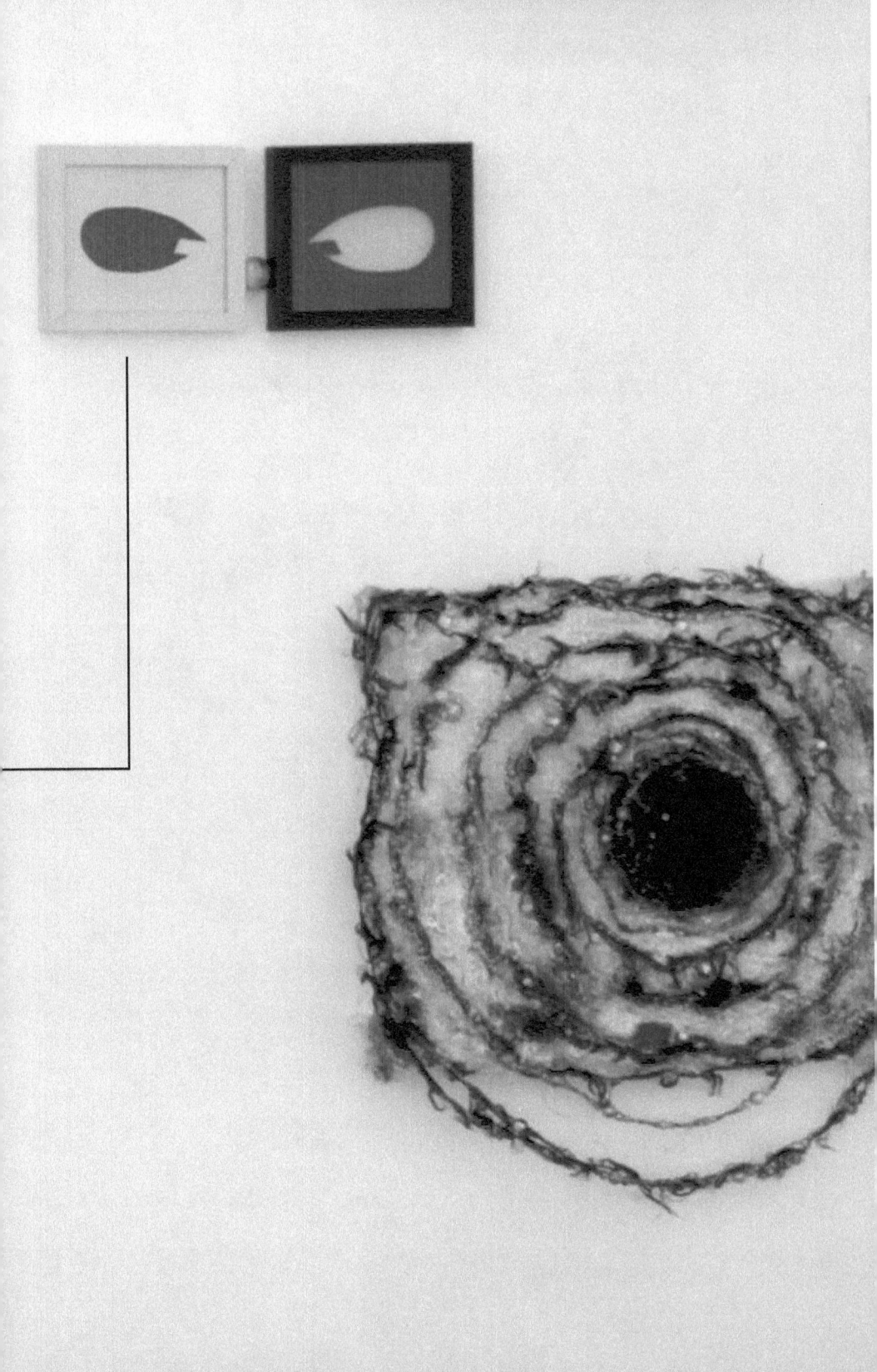

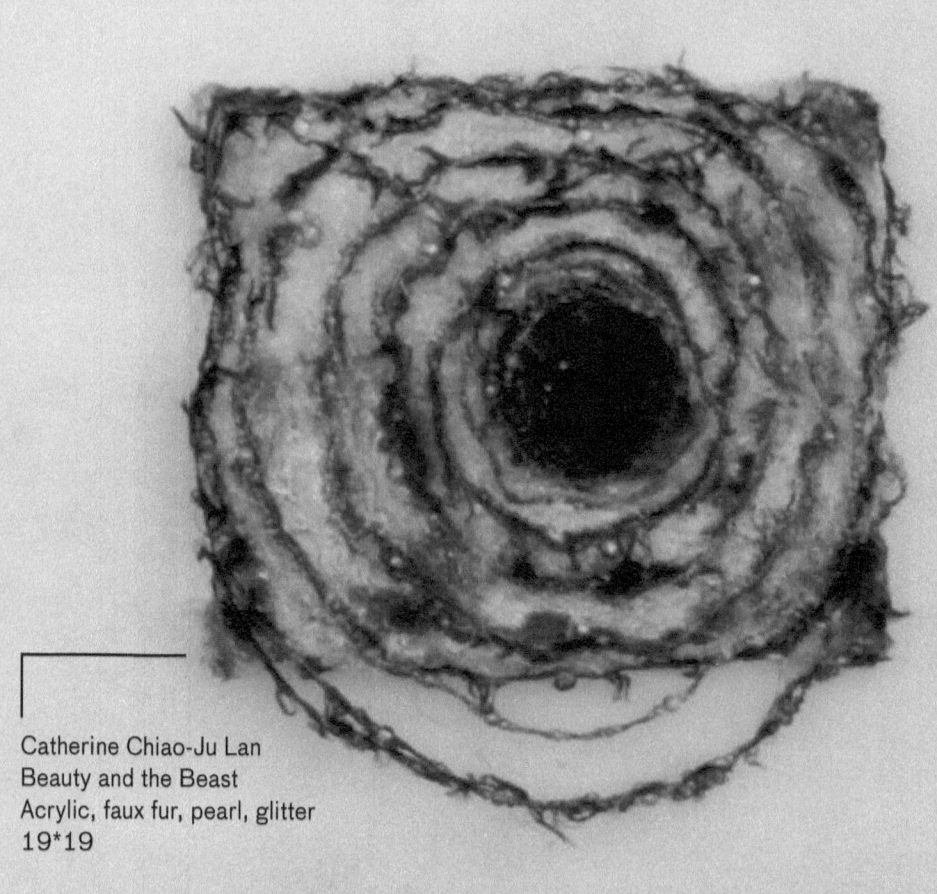

Catherine Chiao-Ju Lan
Beauty and the Beast
Acrylic, faux fur, pearl, glitter
19*19

The material – Faux fur, fox fur, polyester blends, glitter, fluorescent nylons, sequined lace, pearls, glitter, rhinestone and spray paint – reflect contemporary Asian pop culture that is derived from surface and appearance. Using saccharin, candy-like colors, these fabrics are collaged, cut, assemblaged into a painting-relief. The Baroque-style structure deconstructs the pop mythos of classical narrative characters: a princess or prince in Snow White, a bride or groom in Snake Leaves, a wolf or a girl in Little Red Riding Hood. The working process is improvisational and spontaneous, reflects the idea of theatricality and performativity. It is inspired from the idea of shopping and home-décor. I'm interested in appropriating desire from life and from the materialistic world. I continue to explore formal issues of color, texture and composition in painting that belies poignant explorations of female identity.

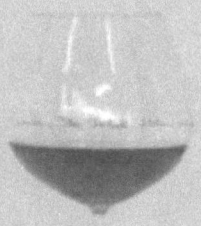

Sarah Butler
A Water
Handwriting on glass and water
5*9.5

No matter how complete the conversion to
virtual realities in our digital era, the concrete
nature of national identity persists. Felt
especially in the collections of documentation
prized by inveterate transnationals proofs
of good faith in photography and letters
national borders are high among the most
actual of myths. The truths ascribed to the
signature likewise parallel the ir/reality of our
differences. Awesomely fragile and incredibly
enduring; dangerous and luxurious, archaic
and contemporary, all imagined, real,
arbitrary and affecting, handwritten text in
some cases seems as basic to human being as
water. Through a background in anthropology
and design, my projects use handwriting to
address shifts in the production of space and
the emerging global art practice enabled by
new media. Language can convey mysteries
as profound, truths as real, as images.

Zeynab Izadyar
Duality
Video
4*3

The bitter part is when you realize that this
is a fake experience, because the reflection
that the eye is seeing is part of the image
light that has not passed through the glasses
and has not reached the eye, and that is why
it is reflected and visible to you.

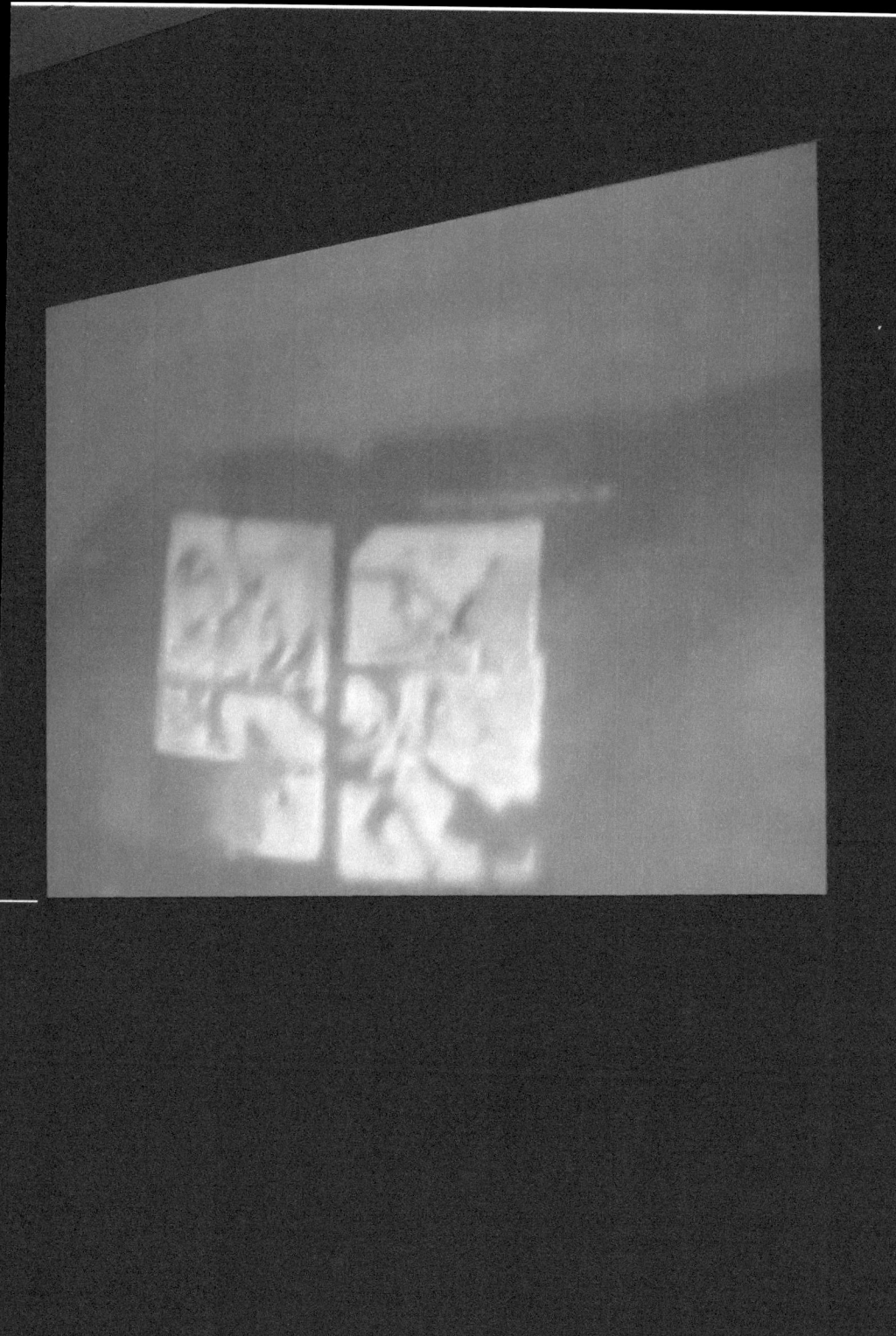

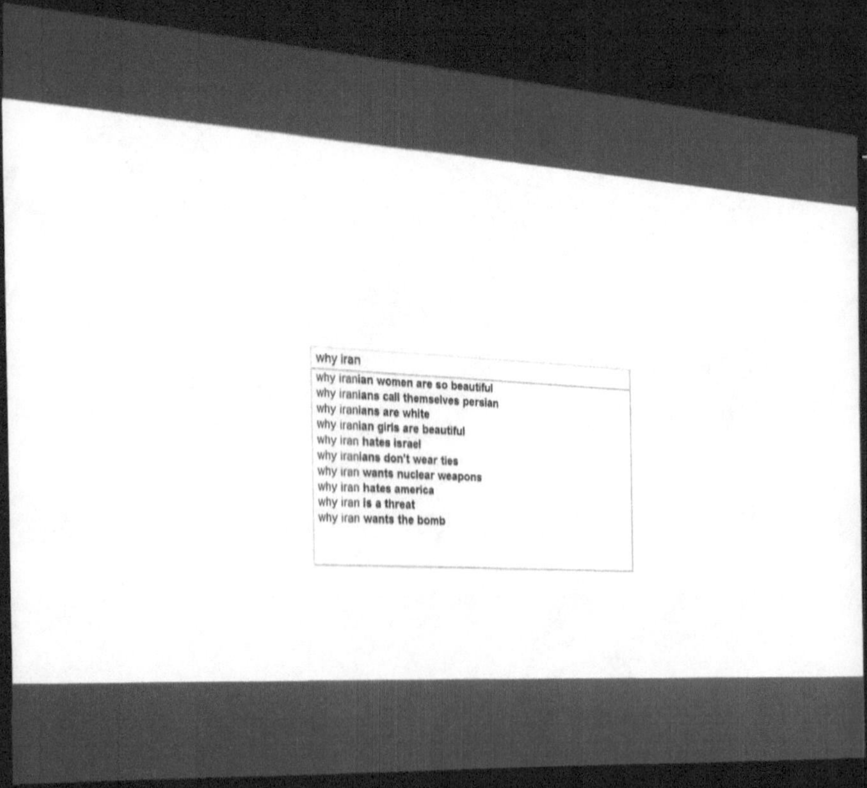
why iran
why iranian women are so beautiful
why iranians call themselves persian
why iranians are white
why iranian girls are beautiful
why iran hates israel
why iranians don't wear ties
why iran wants nuclear weapons
why iran hates america
why iran is a threat
why iran wants the bomb

Gelare Khoshgozaran
WHY
Digital Slideshow
40*22

Why is slideshow that comprises 255 slides. Each slide is a screen capture of an internet page: a blank page with the question(s) most frequently asked about a specific country beginning with the word WHY by the Google Search Engine users. All 255 countries' names were typed in Google search bar following the word Why and the autocomplete results were screen captured. This experiment provides the viewer with an example of the ways in which we exchange information and form our knowledge of the other countries in the world, as it simultaneously reveals the absurdity of this type of common yet questionable means of accessing of information. The irony in the word "why" preceding the countries that are reminiscent of the history of Colonialism was another attraction of these questions for me.

Iliana Ortega
Walk
Video
40*23

My art practice explores how darkness frames light.
To capture images for this exploration, I move slowly
through the nocturnal urban landscape, dedicating
close attention to the workings of artificial light in the
nighttime city and natural light of rural landscape.
By using this technique, I evoke a strong relationship
between the formal elements of photography and
those of drawing – visually relating both to the natural
landscape and exploring how they might reinforce and
complement one another. My ultimate goal in using
these techniques is to uncover the profound relationship
between fiction, representation, and the realty. This
work and research on darkness has led me to seek out
places that provide me with strong natural darkness –
with limited light – creating a mysterious beauty that
equates itself with silence.

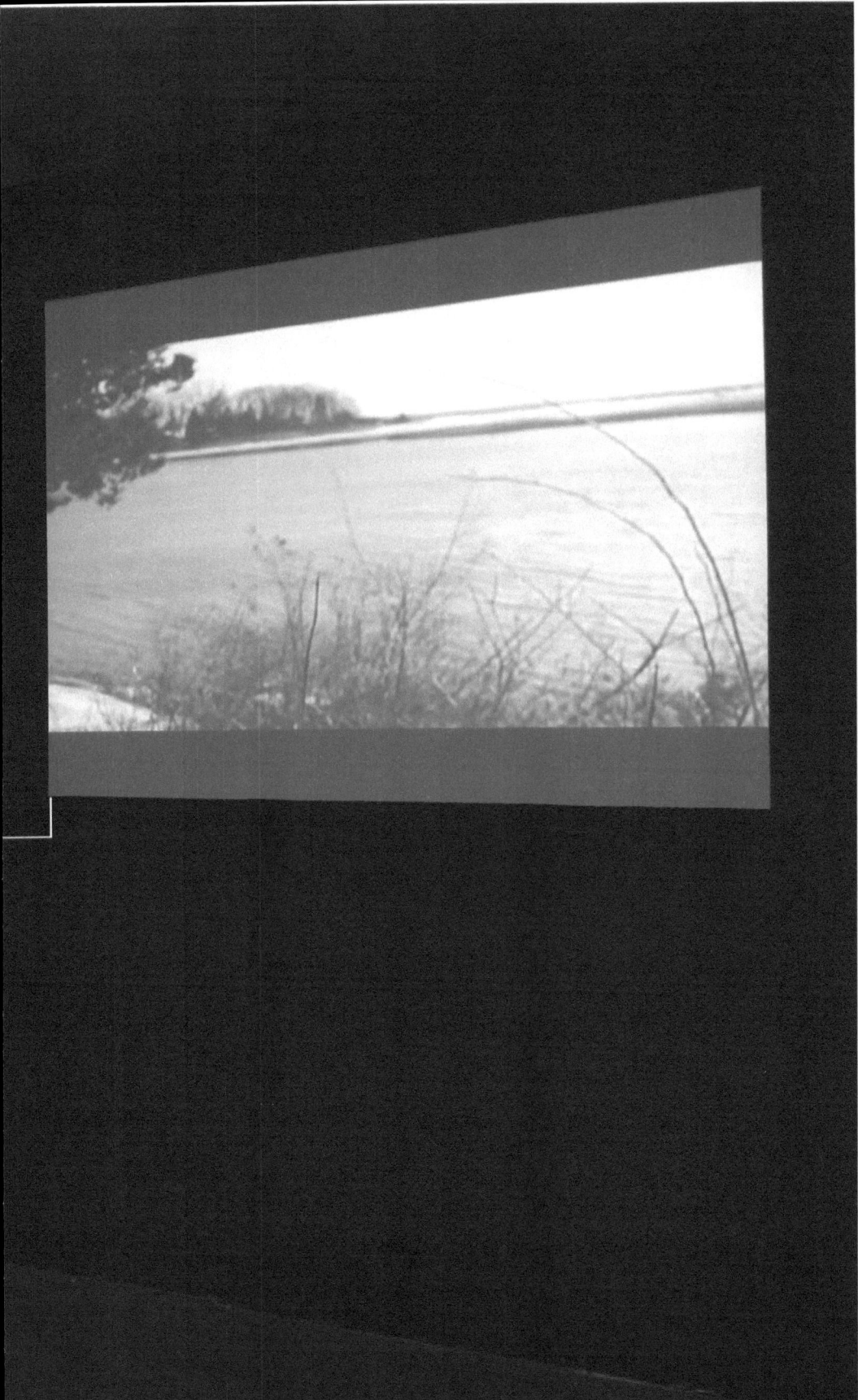

Julie Laenkholm
Eye See You
Video and Video installation
222*222

I made the video installation "Eye see you"
as a comment on the surveillance society we
are living with today. I hope that by visualizing
this discourse, the installation can provide a
perspective that can make us aware of the
political structures our bodies are influenced
by. The limits of what once were private are
now public, and the increasing tendency to
map the bodies of individuals, as well as the
masses of western society, using control
as a tool, is what compelled me to create
the installation as a perspective. With this
perspective I am creating a third space
in order to provide an opportunity for the
viewer to become a participant.

Workshop

When individuals are confronted with large scale administrative problems, a Do-It-Yourself, or a tutorial are not always enough. Instead, we suggest: Do-It-Together! Working together avoids the isolation and muteness that often accompanies international artists throughout their practice. Thus, the purposed events jettison these dismal situations for the opportunities of friendship, mutual aid, and problem solving.

Status! Status! Status! workshop is focused on cooperatively solving the mundane and logistical problems confronting international artists. We want a potluck of information on the process from both professional and personal experience; a moment for sharing tips, hints, tricks and advice among participants. Those involved are encouraged to bring anything which may be helpful. Together we can come to solutions, which are unexpected, innovative and empowering.

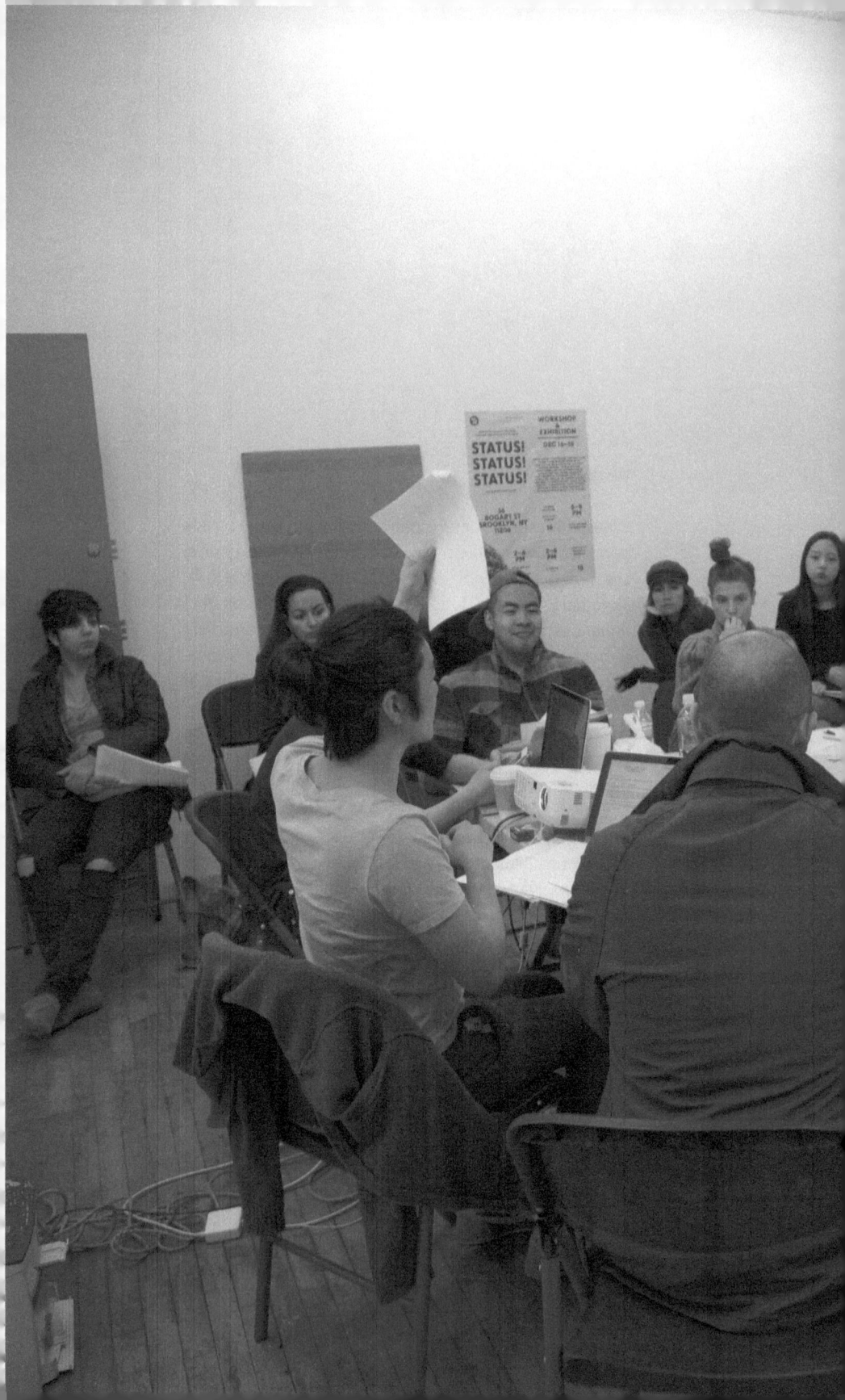

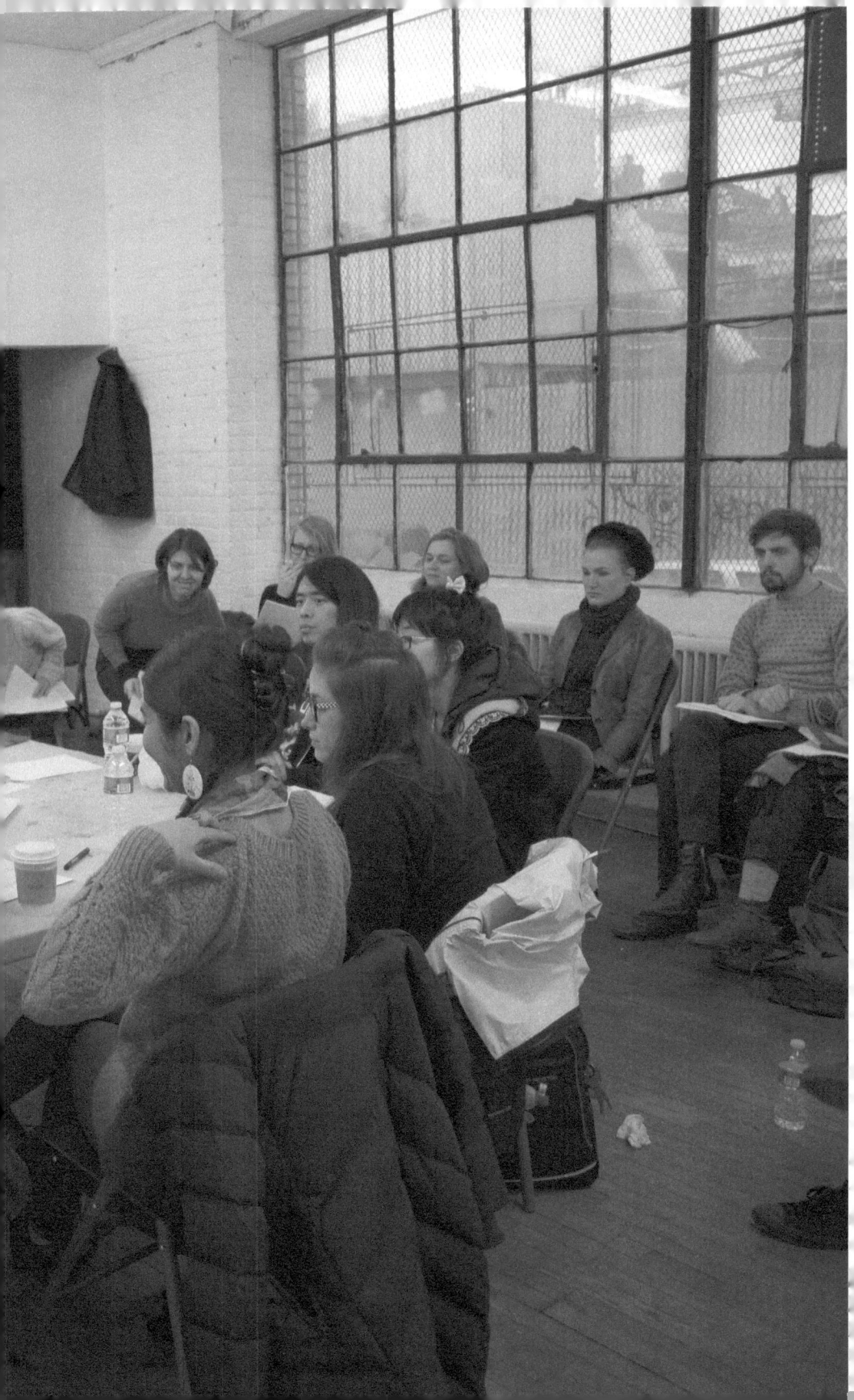

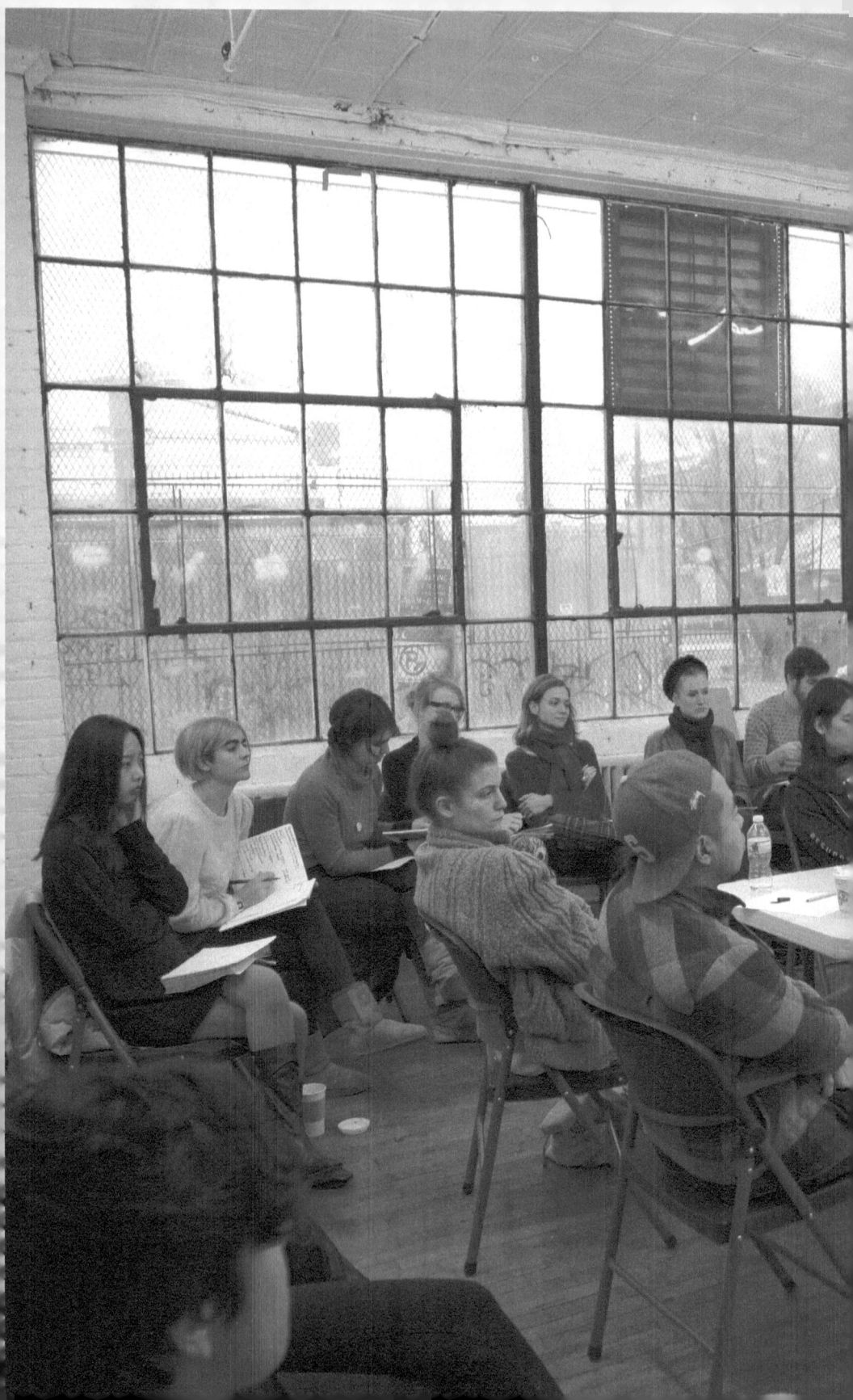

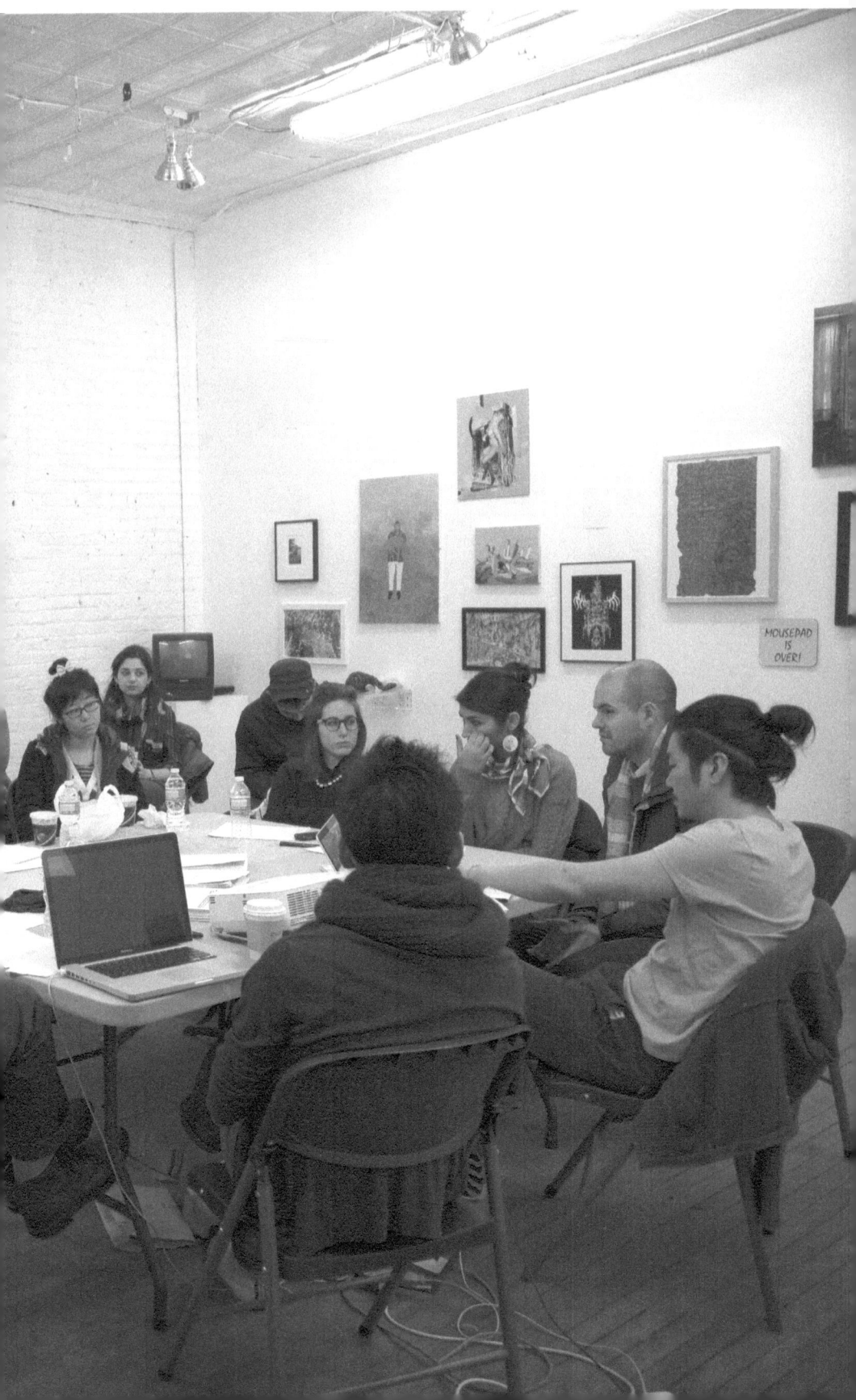

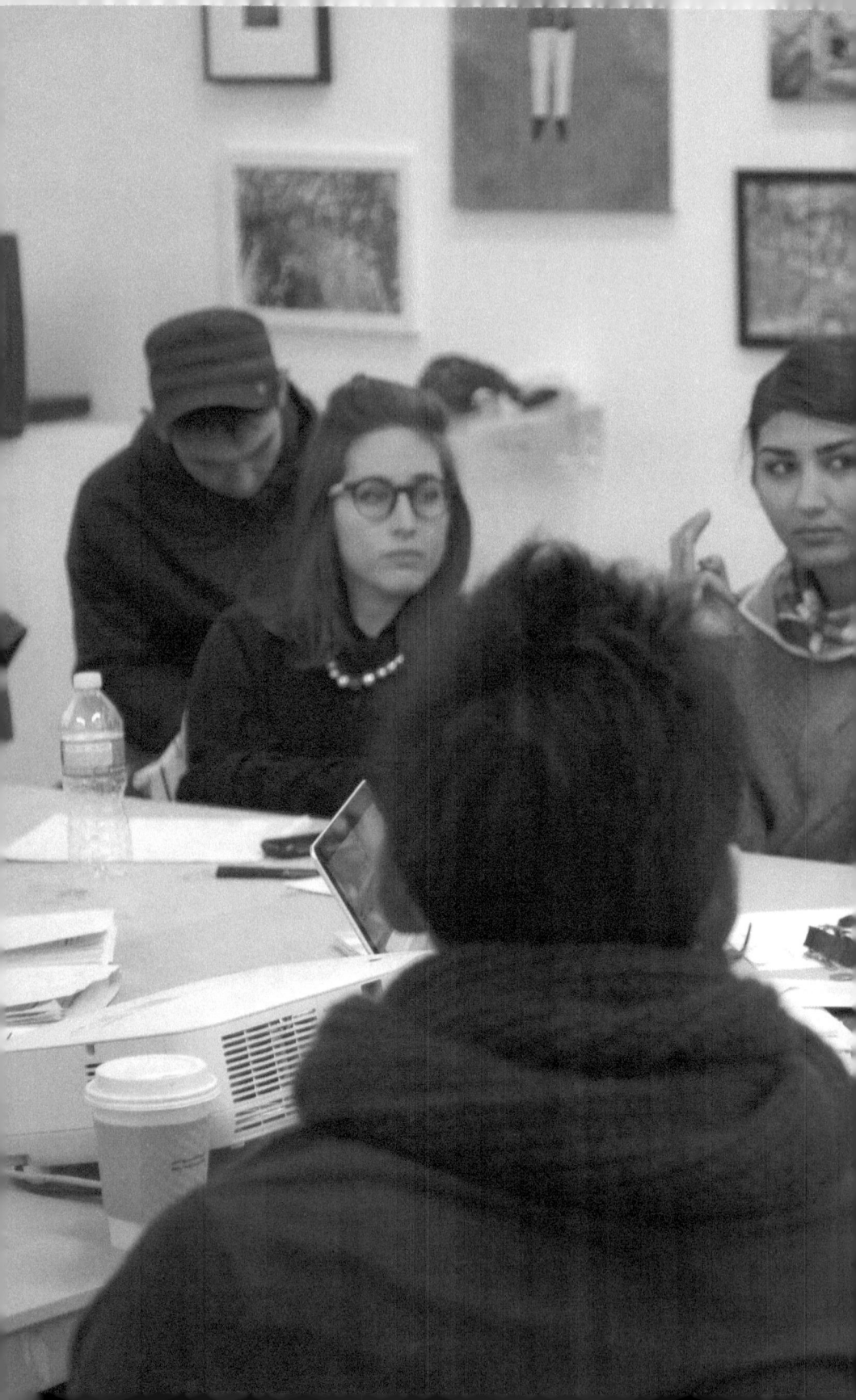

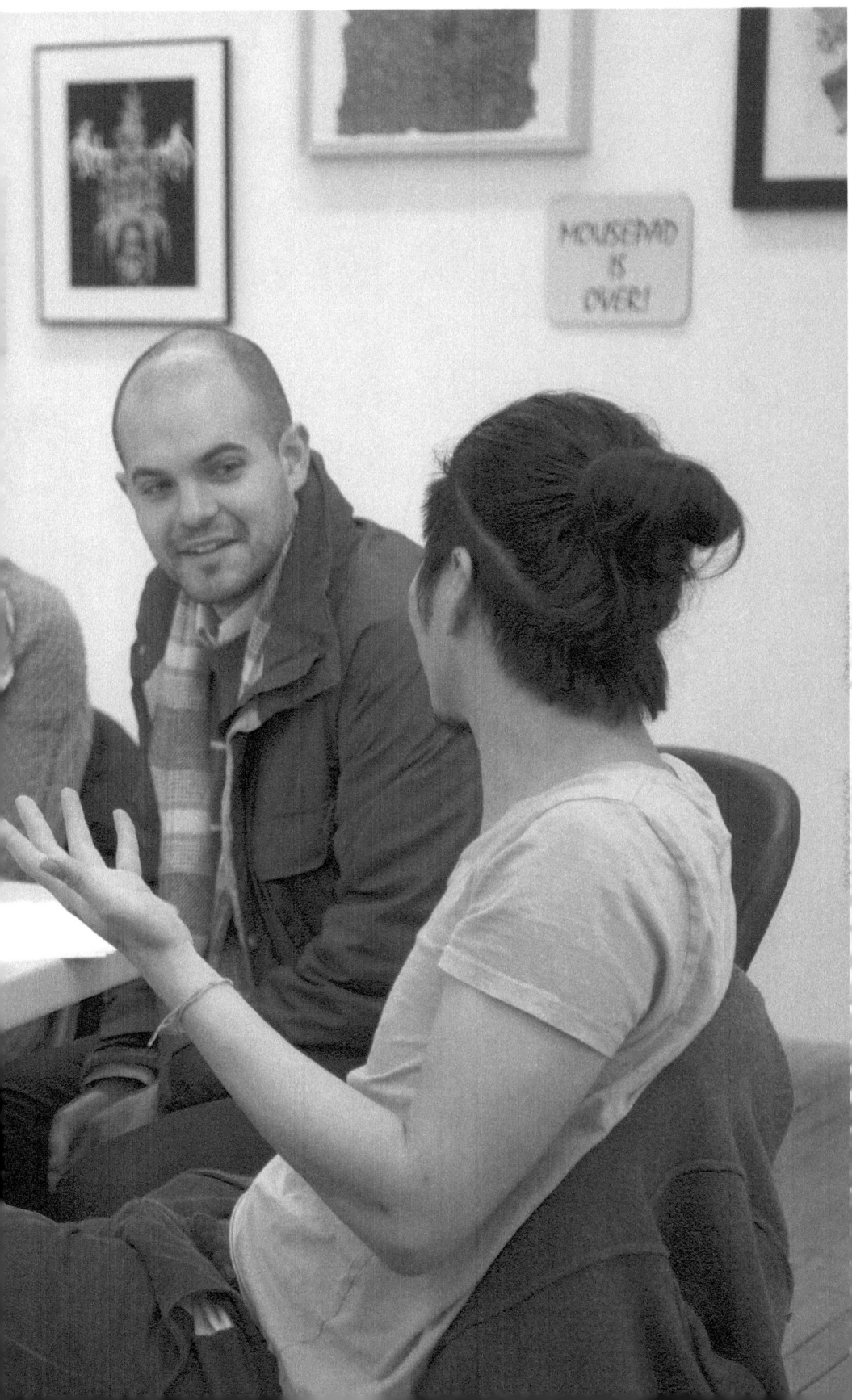

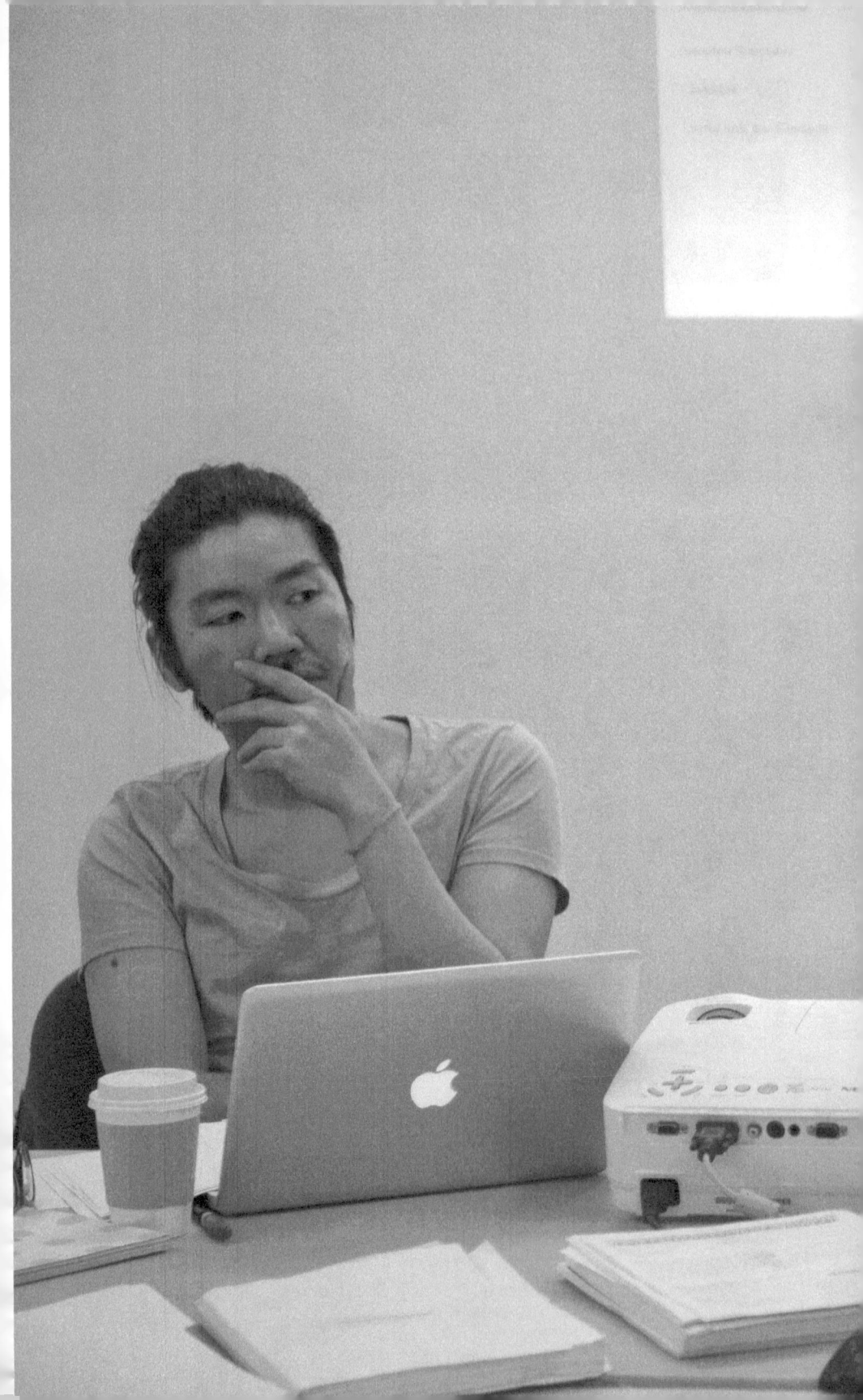

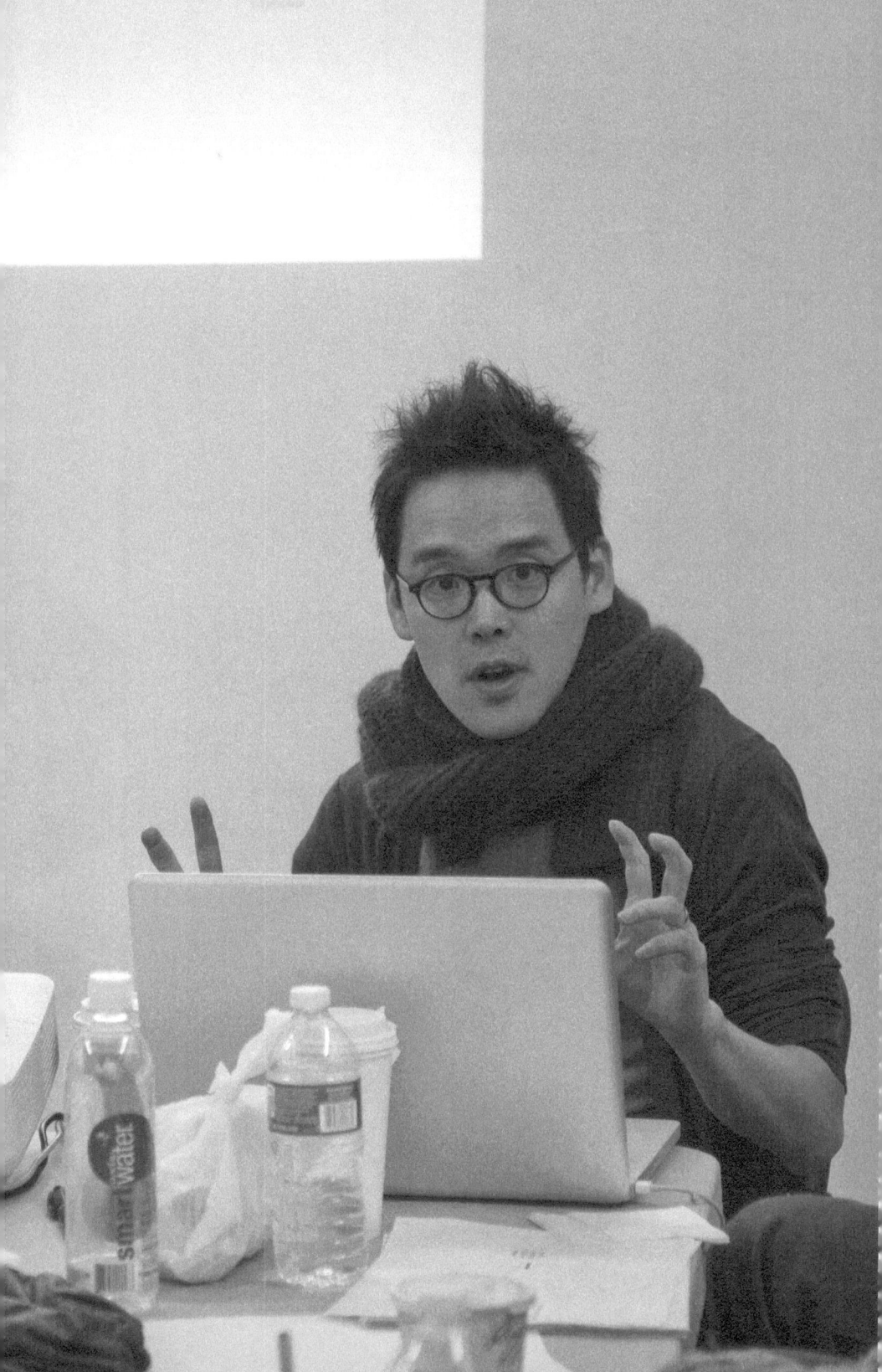

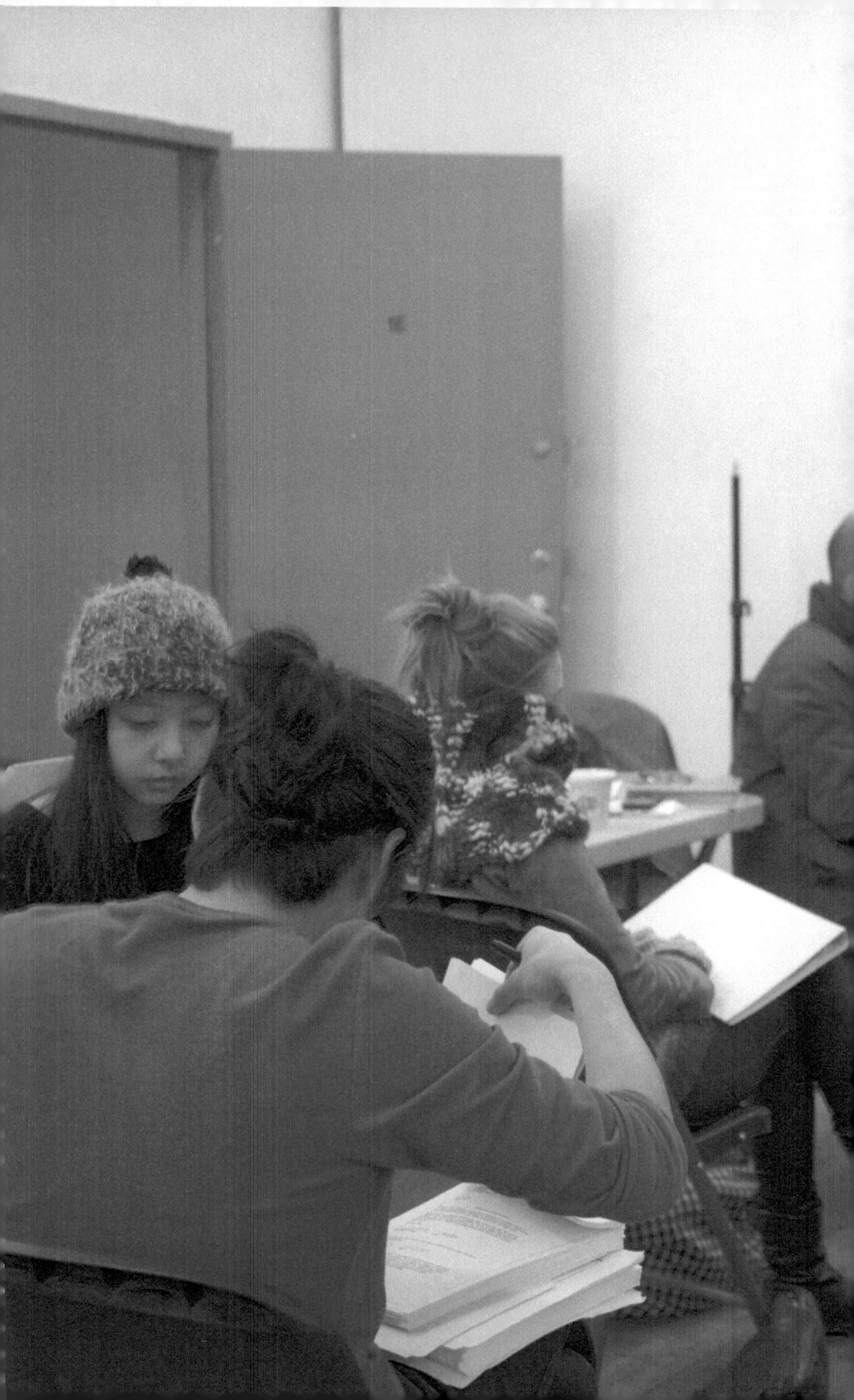

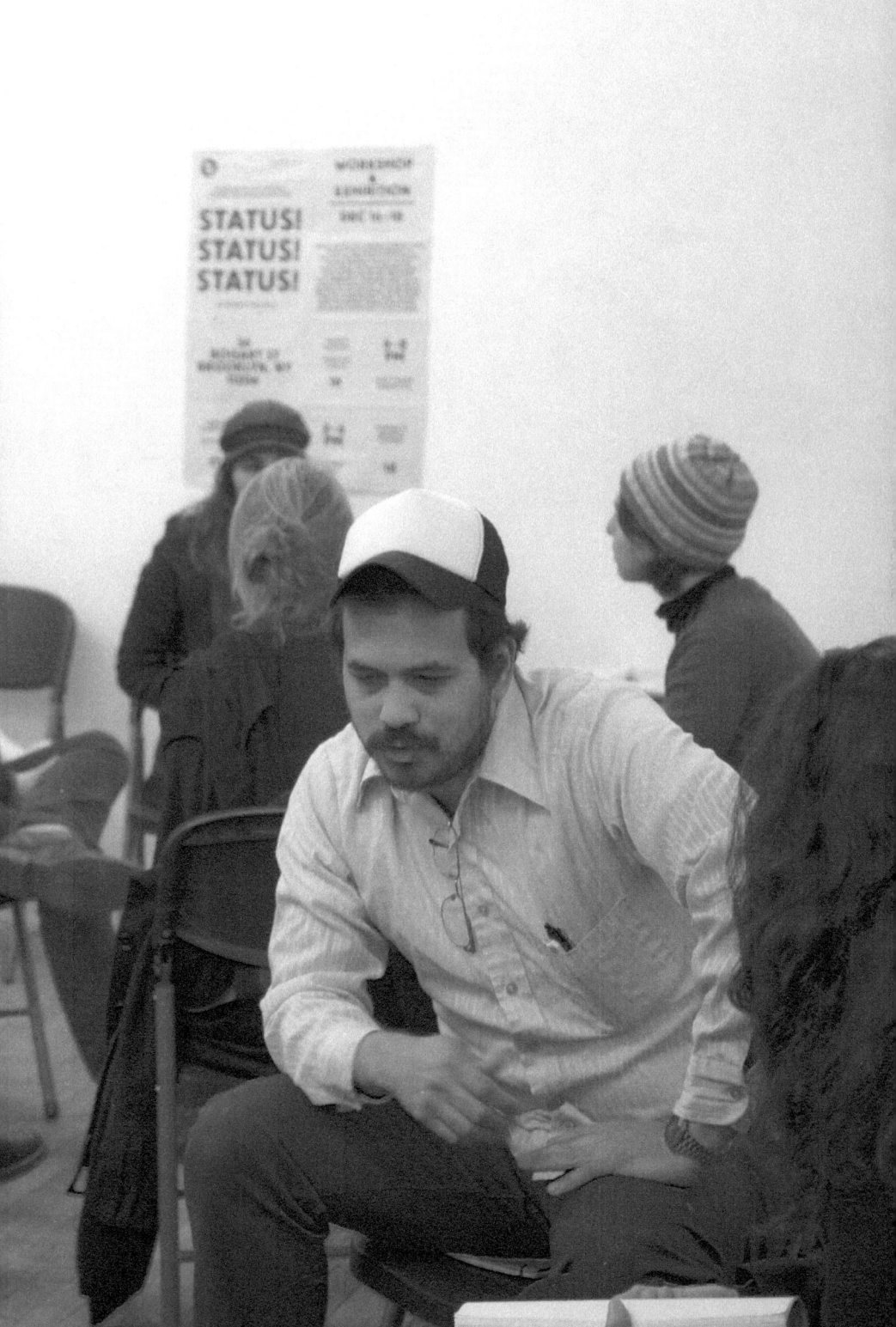

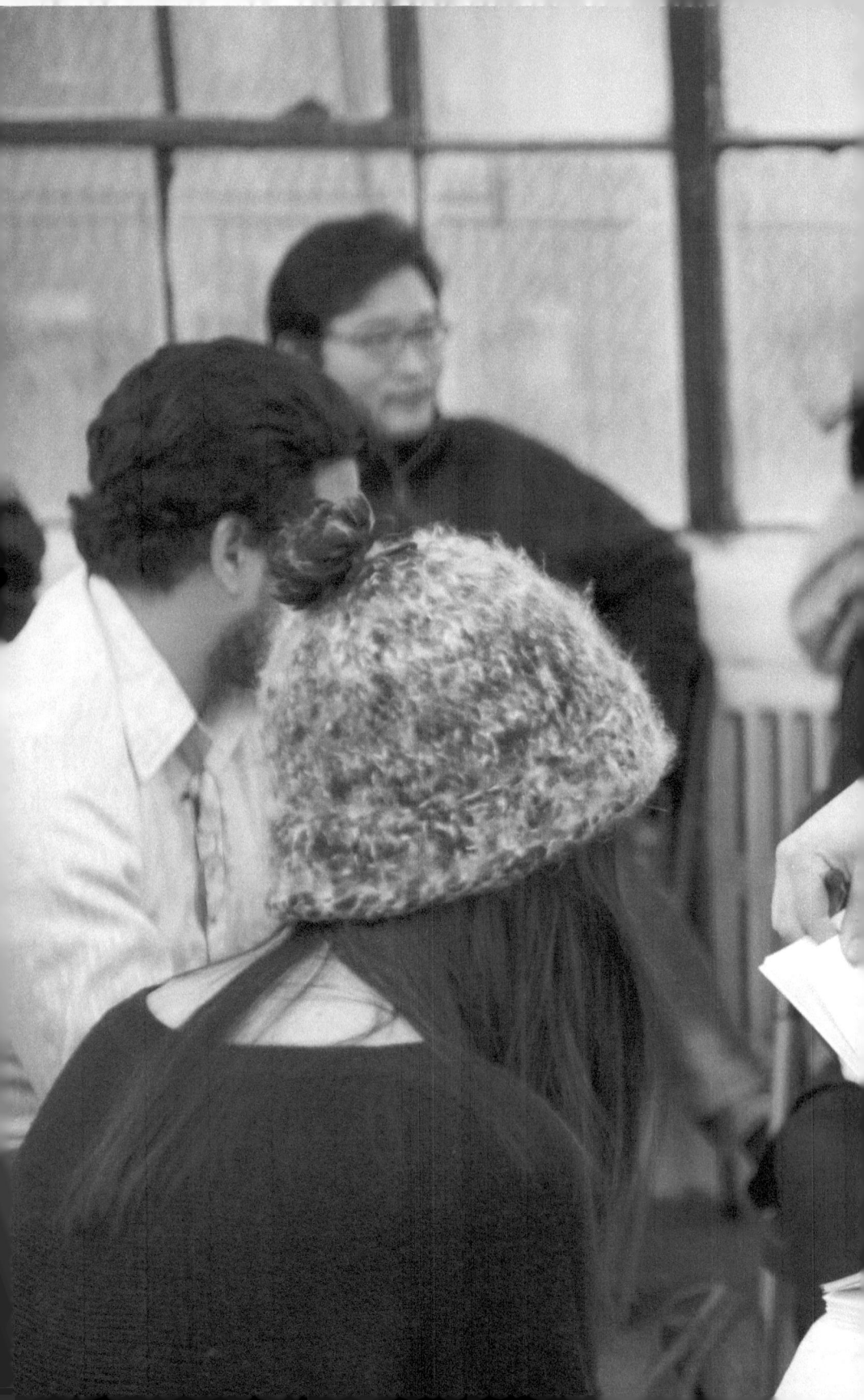

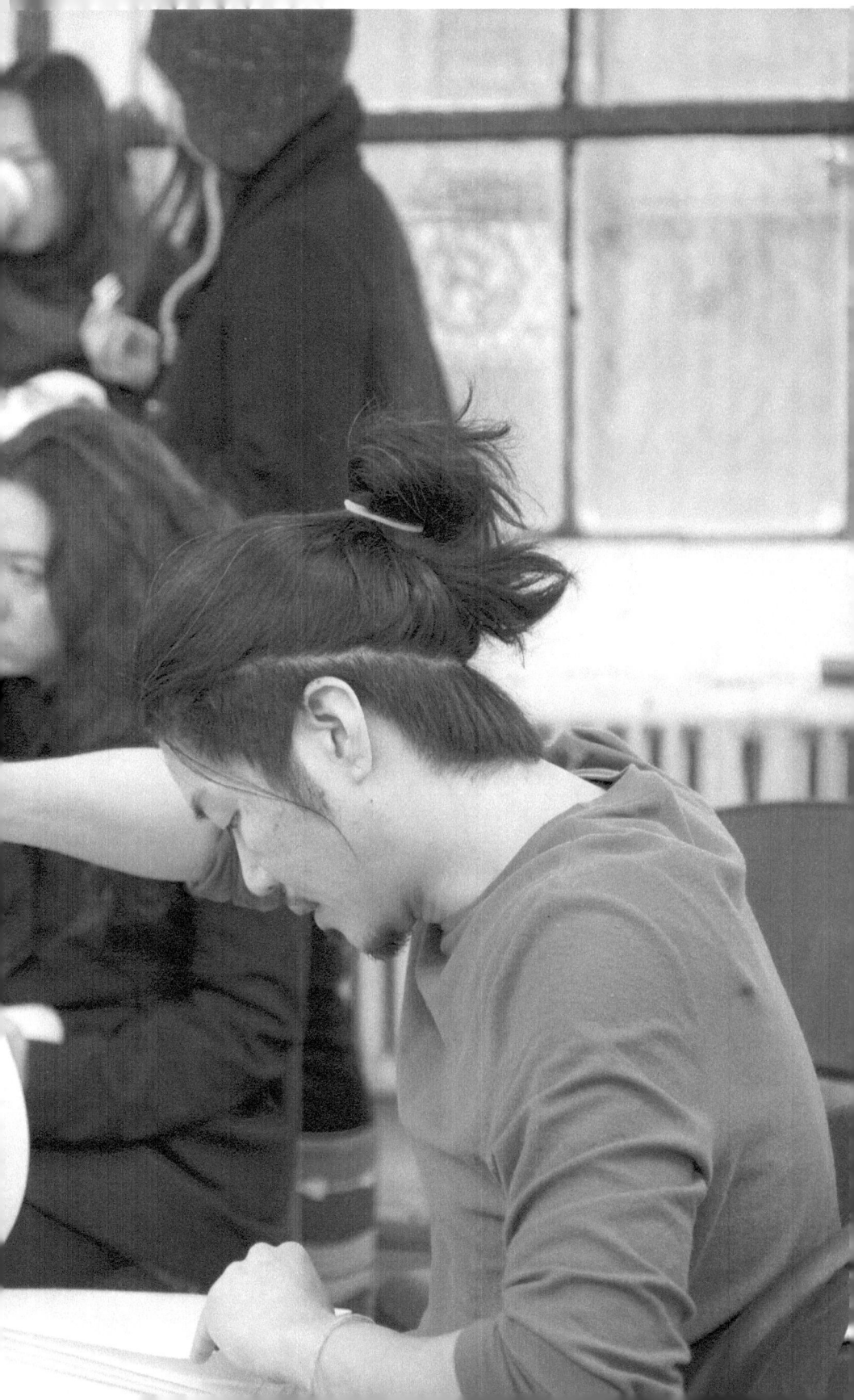

This Publication accompanies the exhibition Status! Status!
Status!, curated by AGWF and presented at Interstate
Projects, Brooklyn, NY, December 16, 2011 - December
18, 2011

First published in the United States of America in 2012 by
Math Practice, LLC.
325 Melrose St. 2L
Brooklyn, NY 11237
www.math-practice.org
Designed by Zeynab Izadyar
www.zeynabizadyar.com

AGWF
56 Bogart St.
Brooklyn, NY 11206
www.ag-wf.com

ISBN
979-1-300-01882-7

  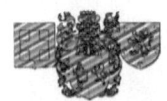

www.ingramcontent.com/pod-product-compliance
Lightning Source LLC
Chambersburg PA
CBHW021927170526
45157CB00005B/2211